The Complete System in Four Parts

Powerful wisdom for positive-thinking men and women: tools, tips and techniques for personal success, happiness, confidence, self-fulfillment and mastery of the art of living, no matter what!

Disclaimer

The matters covered within this publication are the result of considerable research. However, the Publisher and the Author make no warranty or representation regarding the suitability of the material in any individual case. You should use the information and recommendations of this publication at your own risk, adapting its recommendations to suite your own circumstances in the light of common sense. Neither the Author nor the Publisher accept any liability for any damages or losses whatsoever, including, loss of business, revenue, profits, or consequential loss resulting from anyone following any suggestions or recommendations found within this publication. The Reader accepts all responsibility for any decision made as a result of reading this publication. Nothing stated within its pages is to be deemed a valid substitute for legal, accounting, medical or other professional advice. Please do not cease any course of medication in the expectation that following the contents of this guide may take its place. The Reader should regularly consult a physician in matters relating to personal health and particularly with respect to any symptoms that may require diagnosis or medical attention.

The Publisher stresses that the information contained herein may be subject to varying state and/or local laws or regulations. All users are advised to seek competent counsel to determine what state and/or local laws or regulations may apply to the user's particular situation or business. Adherence to all applicable laws and regulations, federal, state, and local, governing professional licensing, business practices, advertising, and all other aspects of doing business in any jurisdiction is the sole responsibility of the Reader. This publication may contain technical inaccuracies and typographical errors. Any perceived slights of specific people or organizations are unintentional.

Have fun with this guide and good luck in all virtuous aspirations.

> *"This book shows you how to unlock your most valuable resource: your own true potential!"*

© Copyright Alan Ackroyd 2017 All rights reserved.

No part of this publication may be reproduced, published or transmitted in any form or by any means electronic, mechanical, photocopying, recording or otherwise without the prior written permission of the Author.

ISBN-13: 978-1507565568
ISBN-10: 1507565569

Success Psychology Society
Adeptican Publishing
F3@Adeptican.com

Printed in the United States of America
Published in Great Britain & North America

Part 1: Chapters 1-7
Dreams, goals and maximizing good fortune

This section covers the groundwork of this amazing formula for personal success: It reveals how to define what you really want from life and prepares you for the life-changing techniques revealed throughout the rest of this book.

Part 2: Chapters 9-15
Conditioning your mind for improved outcomes

This section looks at optimizing your mindscape for success. Your mindscape is the key factor that determines your outcomes and destiny. It reveals the most powerful ways to maximize your inner potential for amazing results.

Part 3: Chapters 16-21
Building wealth and keeping it for long term security

This section focuses primarily on career planning and the development of wealth, though life-changing insights, some of which can be applied in other areas of your life too.

Part 4: Chapters 22-30
Formidable formulas for faster fulfillment

This section covers additional techniques, tips and tactics that will massively accelerate your personal success and ignite your latent powers according to your true and deepest desires.

TABLE OF CONTENTS

Foreword by Dr. Gary Webb 7
Welcome from the Author 9
1. ARE YOU FEELING LUCKY? If not, why might that be? 21
2. LOA vs. GFA Debunking the 'Law of Attraction' 33
3. YOUR INNERMOST DREAMS Give them due consideration! 43
4. THE PERSON YOU'LL BECOME Developing the character 49
5. THE IMPORTANCE of GOALS The linchpin of achievement .. 55
6. A SITUATION-TRANSFORMER Improve life on four fronts 69
7. EXAMINE YOUR HABITS They can make or break you 75
8. SAUCEDARTS Neutralize your worries 89
9. THINKING ABOUT THINKING Optimize your mindscape 101
10. BYPASS THE BOUNCER! & other self-programming tips..... 113
11. CREATIVE THINKING Be a goldmine of winning ideas 123
12. CONTROLLED RELAXATION for multiplied capability.......... 131
13. CONCENTRATION POWER and its dynamic potential 143
14. EMOTIONAL MATURITY & emotional intelligence 157
15. PLUG THOSE KNOWLEDGE GAPS before they sink you!...... 167
16. REFLECTIONS ON WEALTH and the value of money 177
17. CAREER DEVELOPMENT to hasten financial security.......... 187
18. BUILDING WEALTH with exponential growth.................... 199
19. DEBT: A TWO-EDGED SWORD not to be played with 207
20. SUCCESSFUL NEGOTIATING a pivotal success skill.............. 217
21. AN ENTERPRISE OF YOUR OWN Could this be for you? 227
22. DAVID & GOLIATH PRINCIPLE Less effort, better results! .. 243
23. AVOIDING DISTRACTIONS the impediment to progress 249
24. THE IRREPLACEABLE ASSET and how to use it.................... 257
25. IMPROVING VITALITY for increased effectiveness............. 267
26. CHARM & CHARISMA Secrets of personal magnetism 281
27. NON-VERBAL COMMUNICATION Pay attention to it! 293
28. A NETWORK OF SUPPORTERS The non-island approach 303
29. 30+ POWER HABITS to optimize your future 311
30. FINAL THOUGHTS An important decision for you.............. 329

ACKNOWLEDGMENTS

Special thanks to the Success Psychology Society, the Success Secrets Society and Science of Mind UK for helping to make this project a success, and to Fleet Street's Gerry Benson and Robert Ackroyd for editing, proof-reading and constructive feedback. Our gratitude also goes out to Dr Gary Webb of Dalton GA, for strategic support in this project. Thanks also to everyone who provided input during this material's initial testing phase when the original version was published as the *Personal Power Program* from the Success Secrets Society founded by the Author.

Foreword by Dr. Gary Webb

Dr. Gary Webb is the retired US Navy Chaplain, psychotherapeutic counsellor and highly acclaimed author of books about combating addictions and debt.

The author of *Fast-track to Fabulous Fulfillment* assumes that your aspirations are ethical. He has committed himself to giving you the tools to accomplish your greatest dreams. His intent is to liberate you from the failure, frustration, and repeated disappointments that characterize so many lives.

For some, the notion of pursuing self-fulfillment might seem selfish. For this author, that is far from inevitable. Why? Because he has found that being the best you can be can make you into a beacon of hope for others.

Some people measure fulfillment differently than others, sometimes seeing it only regarding outward accomplishments. However, outward progress is related to inward process, changes in thought and emotion. The author guides us through processes that move us upward and forward. Although the progress will not always be what we expected, the process is equipping us for taking another step in the direction of our dreams.

Before we can establish new thought patterns, we must unlearn the faulty ones that have hindered us in the past. The author again guides us into ways to transform our inner monolog toward positive change. One of the best things about this book is the practical assignments. With the help of our guide, we can make steady, if somewhat slow, progress in the right direction.

Although the author writes in a very readable, non-academic style, I was also encouraged by the excellent collection of wise quotations drawn from many cultures and periods of history.

The author's Pyramid Plan Situation Transformer (PPST) is an incredibly simple way to produce a visual image of our goals in four dimensions at a time. I found it much more concise and functional than many that are included in other "success" oriented books.

In another chapter, he gave me some practical steps to banish worry in whatever form it appears in my life. As I read through his material, the insightful perspectives Mr. Ackroyd has gained through years of study and his training in psychotherapy are evident. His ability to communicate profound principles with simplicity and clarity is very valuable for readers.

When I began to consider who might benefit from reading this book, I was stuck. That's the wrong question, even though I usually try to answer it in reviews. This time, the question should be more like, 'Who *won't* benefit from reading this book?' The answer would have to be someone who is completely satisfied with every aspect of their life and is unwilling to change any part of it. Everyone else should find something to enrich their lives — including me!

Welcome from the Author

Dear Reader,

Congratulations on finding this book. You and I have a great deal in common. We are both interested in the most exciting of subjects: that of personal success and fulfillment. I also think you are of above average intelligence, because you have demonstrated the wisdom to invest your time, money and attention where the payoff is potentially the greatest, namely, this book!

Today, there is cause for celebration, because this book you have discovered truly contains the keys to a fabulous new chapter in your life; perhaps a better one than you have imagined. Think of yourself as a gold miner who has just hit the mother lode! The special techniques and insights in this book will change your life in amazing ways, enabling you to actualize dreams and ambitions that you have struggled to make progress towards, plus others that either didn't occur to you before, or that you have shelved, considering them beyond reach.

How this book came into being

Some years ago I founded the *Success Secrets Society* to share, explore and develop techniques for self-improvement. With the help of my most accomplished members, I developed an exclusive home study course to teach the best techniques yet discovered during 40+ years of keen interest in self-development methodology. That course proved to be exceptionally popular and successful - and what you now hold in your hands is a new, and further-improved version of that course, revised and expanded for the 21st century. My involvement and training in psychotherapy gave me new insight into the way the mind works and why many people often lead such unsatisfactory lives. This is what prompted me to further develop the course material and present it in the form of a book, available to everyone, who, like you, has the insight to recognize its potential.

Who this book is for

Assuming your aspirations are ethical, this unique and powerful book is definitely for YOU! It is ideally suited to people of all ages and all genders. You can use it to massive advantage in whatever aspect of life you want to excel in: everyday living, business, money-making, entrepreneurship, creativity, academia, sports, social success, you name it.

You have what it takes

Because you are reading these words now, I already know that you have what it takes to benefit fabulously from this material and achieve incredible success and self-fulfillment according to your own unique wishes. This book is the catalyst that will ignite your true potential and improve your circumstances radically. Perhaps you have some disadvantages that make the achievement of your wishes seem more than a little challenging. At the same time, you have probably noticed that some of the most disadvantaged people alive have achieved phenomenal levels of happiness and fulfillment despite the apparent odds. No matter how bad your present situation, the keys to profound change and phenomenal improvement await you in this book.

Easy reading

Each chapter of this book is a comfortable bite-sized chunk of powerful guidance that may stimulate your thinking about your own situation and mindscape and give you insights about new and better ways to move your life to the next level. Each chapter requires only a short session to read because it contains no waffle or padding, and no tedious case studies. It will be a catalyst that will open up phenomenal scope for positive changes in your life.

The ultimate rescue plan

"Most men lead lives of quiet desperation" wrote Henry David Thoreau. I hope you are not one of them, but even if you are, this book can transform your life when you implement its guidance. Even the first edition of this book did that – and this edition is even more powerful! Failure, frustration and repeated disappointments can take their toll on one's wellbeing. That, in turn, can affect one's relationships and give rise to impressions that one doesn't have what it takes. Before long, one can find oneself in a motivational nose-dive, in desperate need of a rescue plan. This book is the ultimate rescue plan!

Welcome to the ecstatic zone!

Unlike other self-improvement programs, this one does not demand that you kiss your comfort zone goodbye! Pause and imagine for a moment how it will feel to actualize your most compelling dreams and ambitions. It feels fantastic, doesn't it? Entering a victorious new life of fresh hope, success and sublime happiness is *more* than just *comfortable*; you'll *feel ecstatic!* Consider this book not as just your new *comfort zone* but as your new ECSTATIC ZONE!

This book will be a crucial resource for you in the months and years ahead. You will notice your life improving even while you are digesting the first chapter. You can soon outdo your competition, achieve the dreams you shelved, and impress those who care about you. All you need to do is continue reading and reflecting, assimilating and implementing, and your success is **guaranteed**! As you read this material at your own comfortable pace, with full attention, you may soon notice new feelings of inner peace, hope and ambition kindling within you and this is just a hint of what's in store.

Is self-fulfillment selfish?

No, not necessarily! By being the best you can be, you become a beacon of hope to others. You'll gain the increasing respect and admiration of your loved ones and you'll become a guiding light for those with aspirations comparable to yours - and the world needs good role models! You may notice your happiness increasing as you read this material, and this will positively affect everyone you meet. When you adopt the amazing techniques and insights from this book, you will become a better person in many ways. So congratulations; you are on the right track now! And NOW is the best time there will ever be to get these powerful tools into your tool kit so you can be ahead of the game and start living like never before! This book guides you in the direction that is right for YOU, with speed, power and ease hitherto unknown.

Claim your birthright

Personal fulfillment is your birthright. So let's take advantage of the most powerful techniques available to achieve it! This book reveals these techniques. You can gain massive advantages from them, regardless of your age, nationality, sex or religion. Whether your vision of success is one of material wealth, social success, moral virtue, academic, artistic or scientific genius, or becoming a world-class lover, this book is the golden key that will unlock your future! As you follow its guidance with full focus and an open mind, the rewards will be incalculable!

Imagine...

Pretend you are already well into this book and enjoying the rewards of having multiplied powers and capabilities. You may already get a sense of how that will feel. It feels wonderful, doesn't it? Do you already have an idea of how you will want to deploy your new powers and capabilities? Perhaps some of your core ambitions are still rising to the surface of your awareness. If so, you will form a much clearer picture of what you want from life before you are half way through this book. As you read on, you'll increasingly realize the fantastic possibilities opening up to you.

A force for good

For your own sake and for the sake of everyone else, please only ever use this book's techniques for good and ethical purposes. They can backfire on anyone who tries to use them for immoral purposes, or whose motives are

malicious, vindictive or irresponsible. So please use them wisely and honorably!

Progressing through this book

Each chapter of this book is a bite-sized helping. An ideal rate at which to proceed is to read and implement one chapter a day. It is better to consider each chapter thoroughly and in depth than to skim through several in one sitting without fully implementing its recommendations. It is preferable to set aside a specific time of the day for each reading and the contemplation of each chapter and to make plans according to its recommendations. Choose a time when you are mentally alert, and undistracted.

Four Parts

I have organized the chapters of this book into four parts or sections. I recommend completing each section in turn. The four parts are:

Part 1: Dreams, Goals and Good fortune

Part 2: Configuring your Mind for Success

Part 3: Wealth; Ways to Get it and Increase it

Part 4: Formidable Formulas for Faster Fulfillment

Ideally, you should start at the beginning with Part 1, and continue steadily through to the end of Part 4. This will ensure that you have taken in the material in the intended order, for optimal results.

If you find that any chapter is definitely not relevant to your own unique situation, then feel free to skip to the next chapter. It is possible that one or more of the ideas in this book may be familiar to you. That's okay because it is important to be reminded of certain principles and have them expressed in fresh ways. Other ideas in this book will be new to you and will expand your general aptitudes in fabulous ways. And we won't be sharing dubious ideologies such as the alleged 'law' of attraction, which so many people have been disappointed by. Instead, we'll cover proven approaches to self-betterment that are easy, yet truly reliable!

Now, a brief flying lesson!

When I was a small boy, a pal of mine tried to convince me that he knew how to fly without any mechanical aid! I implored him to share his secret. He intimated: "It's easy; you jump into the air and before you land, you jump again... Keep repeating this, and up and away you fly!" While the idea of soaring through the clouds like Superman certainly had its appeal, I wasn't really convinced! However, I think I may have attempted it (just to make sure)! Alas, either I didn't have the knack, or Newton's Law was refusing to play ball!

As I grew older though, I discovered that this technique of jumping again before you come back to earth has some profoundly beneficial applications in the realm of the mind and the art of living. Imagine for a moment that your goal is not to fly physically, but to sail skywards in terms of, say, self respect, morale, dexterity, social status or physical health, by engaging with one of the following:

- a new and exciting hobby
- a new social group
- a profitable new venture
- a health goal of some kind (and achieving it)

Any of the above will give your morale a boost and your brain something fresh and nourishing to digest. However, all such benefits tend to have a peak point where the payoff for you is highest. Potential benefits are often still there after this point, but when the novelty factor has gone, there is often a tendency to sink back into our old mindset and cease to fully benefit from the new activity. The degree to which we actually benefit could be plotted on a chart, which would follow a curve, like the famous 'bell curve' (so-called because of its shape) that maps the typical life cycle and profitability of products on the market.

Eventually, the plotted line returns to its original level - just like the jumping boy returning to earth, despite all attempts to maintain an upward trajectory! However, here is a key tactic we can employ: we can use the elevation gained from Activity-1 as a springboard to higher elevations through Activity-2, and so on.

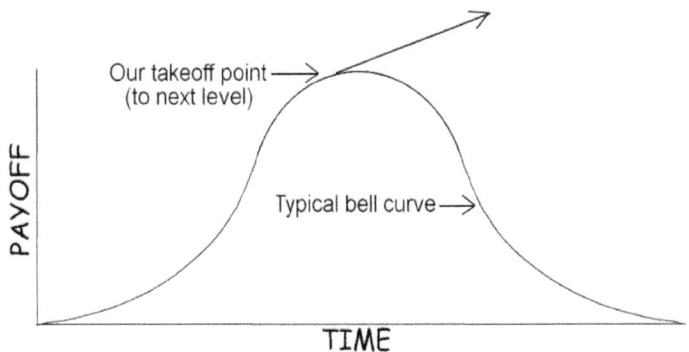

You can apply this very technique to this book. Each chapter will propel you upwards, in capability and potential. Before you lose altitude, each subsequent chapter will take you even higher. Likewise, each of the four parts of this book will take you in four giant leaps towards a shining new future. By the time you reach the end of the book, you should be safely airborne!

Your A-Log (Adeptican Logbook): your first action step!

In this book, you will find many special *Recommended Action Steps* at the end of the chapters. Many of these are simple note-making tasks. In order to be well organized, your first important task is to acquire a notebook, exclusively for recording and modifying your ideas related to this program. This will ideally be a loose-leaf ring binder with plenty of pre-punched ruled pages. Some tabbed divider sheets will help to keep the logbook organized. This will be your all-important *Adeptican Logbook*, (**A-Log** for short; that's how we will refer to it throughout the book). 'Adeptican' and 'Adepticanics' are words I coined, being combinations of the words 'adept' and 'I can' and 'mechanics'.

Your A-Log will play a vital role in this program, so please do not omit this step!

When selecting your ring-binder, consider choosing a color that seems personally significant or positive to you. To make the program more attractive, you could even use colored paper for the pages. It's up to you—do whatever makes your A-Log feel personal and significant to you. Besides the note-making Action Steps, we encourage you to make other notes in your A-Log, however please use it exclusively for matters pertaining closely to this program and your personal journey to success and self-fulfillment. Keeping a record of the benefits and achievements you enjoy along the way is also a great idea.

Consider the contents of your A-Log strictly personal. It is usually best to keep it private because other people's input can cloud the waters and dilute your success potential.

❖ *The No.1 reason people fail in life is because they listen to their friends, family, and neighbors.—Napoleon Hill*

If you share your ideas and plans with the wrong people, they may subtly sabotage your ideas, even unintentionally.

So, without further ado, let us open the throttle now and prepare to take our first glimpse of the blue skies beyond the clouds above the fresh, clear runway ahead...

Claim Your Birthright Now!

DREAMS, GOALS AND GOOD FORTUNE

The first part of the program is primarily about clarifying exactly what you want from life and the changes you want to enjoy. If you are already very clear about this, then you are off to a head start! You will find this key part of the book important and valuable for clarifying and reassessing your goals, dreams and ambitions and exploring additional ones that may provide self-fulfillment in years to come – ones you can prepare for early!

Part One is the fundamental base from which we start. It's your launch pad! Through it, you will develop and crystallize plans to which you can apply the teachings of this complete program for phenomenal results. You will map out your path ahead so you can reach your chosen destinations with optimal efficiency and speed with the true satisfaction you deserve.

❖ *Humanity has the stars in its future, and that future is too important to be lost under the burden of juvenile folly and ignorant superstition. —Isaac Asimov*

1
ARE YOU FEELING LUCKY?
IF NOT, WHY MIGHT THAT BE?

❖ *It is the mark of an inexperienced man not to believe in luck.*
—Joseph Conrad

To make optimal progress on the supremely exciting task of making the most of life, it makes sense to ensure that we proceed under conditions that are as favorable as possible. Most of this book is designed to optimize your luck, and improve your outcomes, and in this chapter we will start to consider ways to improve our fortune.

❖ *Concerning all acts of initiative or creation, there is one elementary truth...that the moment one definitely commits oneself, then Providence moves too. All sorts of things occur to help one that would otherwise never have occurred. A whole stream of events issues from the decision, raising in one's favor all manner of incidents and meetings and material assistance which no man would have believed would have come his way.* —William Hutchison Murray

One of the first and most important aspects of personal success and fulfillment that we should consider is the subject of what is commonly called 'luck'. This factor plays massive part in determining our degree of success or failure. Fortunes are made by being in the right place at the right time, seemingly by chance. Indeed, being in the right place at the right time can sometimes be worth more than years of hard work or years of effort in becoming educated or trained in a vocational skill. So any way we can influence our own 'luck' should be of paramount interest. Can we have any influence over our luck? Many readers will be surprised to hear that we definitely can, and without magic or the occult!

What is luck?

As everyone knows, 'good luck' is the term we use when things seem to go our way—when events drop into place enabling our hopes to materialize. What we should investigate is what attracts good luck. Many people assume that luck is a matter of pure chance. And much of the time, it does—but often, there is more to it than that. Indeed, the very word 'luck' hints at an underlying intuitive understanding that there is more to it than pure random chance. Most of us can remember times when luck (good or bad) seemed to mysteriously come in gluts. Most of us have experienced being 'on a roll'. Conversely, unfortunate events have occurred, one after another on a day that seemed to be jinxed. And many of us have experienced 'beginner's luck'.

What is not always appreciated is how much we actually attract our 'luck' (good or bad).

How much good luck are you overlooking?

The common view of good luck is that of chance events that befall us when fate goes our way, but there is an alternative view to consider: We are continuously surrounded by, and immersed in, good luck, but the amount of it that we recognize or take advantage of depends on how receptive or 'open' we are to it. The average person encounters hundreds of amazing opportunities every day to which he is oblivious because his mind is absorbed in some pessimistic mood or train of thought, or is in a pessimistic or cynical mindset.

Cognitive scientists now tell us that we filter out about 80-90% of the sensory input we receive, because if we didn't, our minds would be overloaded. They call it 'sensory gating'. The nature of the remaining 10%-20% of input that we actually register, mentally, is largely governed by our state of mind, our mood and the contents of our subconscious mental processes. Whether we perceive fortunate or adverse events is largely determined by the degree to which we are predominantly thinking with patterns of fear, worry, pessimism and self-pity; or positive patterns of hope, expectation, appreciation and optimism.

Is the human race your ally?

When our pursuits are in harmony with the true and universal interests of the human race, we have the entire human race as our ally on some level, and what a formidable ally to have! Suddenly you have over seven billion friends! That's an incredibly large network of supporters! This is one way we can attract 'good luck'. If our activities and pursuits are against these universal human interests, we naturally attract 'bad luck' because the whole world and our subconscious overseer is against us. Swimming against the moral tide is hard, thankless, soul-destroying work, and it gains us nothing of true value—except perhaps teaching us a lesson in how not to live!

We all have a sense of these fundamental universal values. Most people instinctively know good from bad, right from wrong, wholesomeness from depravity; in other words what is in our higher interests and what isn't. At least, the more intelligent among us do. In a nutshell, these higher values reflect what is good for the human race, and our children and our planet on which we and our children rely for survival and comfort.

❖ *Certainly one of the highest duties of the citizen is a scrupulous obedience to the laws of the nation. But it is not the highest duty. —Thomas Jefferson*

Higher Law

Ultimately, all living creatures have the same ultimate interests and values. As human beings, it is in our common interest to survive and to avoid exploitation, enslavement and disease. And all normal people want such a future for their loved ones. In order to function optimally and to live effectively, our own code of living should promote and harmonize with these underlying interests of humanity. Acting in any way that undermines these underlying crucial interests is going against what we might call Higher Law for the sake of simplicity. Such actions or behavior erodes the foundations of civil harmony and peace, such as the fundamental human need for trust, goodwill and security.

Such actions or behaviors include such things as:

- Aggression and offense (physical or psychological)
- Stealing—and not just stealing of material things
- Lying and deceit

It's important to consider that even a thought alone can contravene this Higher Law. Thoughts repeated become habits which beget attitudes that beget more of the same type of thoughts, which sooner or later are articulated. We should never underestimate the power of a spoken or written word.

> *A careless word may kindle strife,*
> *A cruel word may wreck a life,*
> *A bitter word may hate instill,*
> *A brutal word may even kill,*
> *A gracious word may smooth the way,*
> *A joyous word may light the way,*
> *A timely word may lessen stress,*
> *A loving word may heal and bless.*
> —Author unknown

Higher Law's penalty system

Regarding the above verse you might ask who the victim is that it refers to. Whose life might be wrecked by a cruel word you might utter? Whose life might be damaged by a kindly word you might whisper? Certainly it could be someone else's fate that you might change, but ultimately it is also your own—because Higher Law has an in-built penalty system. If we do harm to someone else, we ultimately harm ourselves; we are all so intimately connected by the continuous sea of communication in which we all live. Indeed the old adage: 'what goes around comes around' (or 'what you put out is what you get back') is much more factual than one might assume. The more we lose alignment with Higher Law, the more we have to lie to ourselves that we are behaving justifiably, and the consequence is a loss of connection with our truest and deepest values, and an erosion of our awareness and intelligence.

Who is actually policing the world, according to Higher Law? The answer is *the citizens of Planet Earth!* We do it consciously and subconsciously. Our own subconscious mind possesses great knowledge and wisdom—including an inbuilt understanding of the importance of Higher Law; so much so, in fact that it takes care to punish us, in our own best interests, and the interests of the planet when we contravene it. Every time we go against Higher Law, it places a black mark in our unwritten balance book—a black mark for which we will sooner or later pay the penalty. Sometimes our transgressions bounce right back at us instantly, as in so-called 'instant karma', and sometimes it doesn't happen for a while. In those cases, we often don't make the connection when it happens. One is left wondering: "Why on earth did I have such a bad stroke of luck?" It is just the subconscious mind deciding that we are due for some book-balancing!

Our internal policeman (or shepherd, if you prefer) takes a particularly dim view of any adverse behavior that could multiply its detrimental effects though being copied or emulated by others. And let's face it, humans are notorious for behaving like sheep at times. So setting a bad example to others is a particularly woeful transgression. Thankfully, most people have a conscience, though people are very good at turning a blind eye to it in order to continue with misguided, self-defeating behavior.

Gaining the support of our subconscious helper

So in order to be happy and successful, we really need to have our own subconscious mind on our side. How we feel about ourselves, consciously and subconsciously plays a massive part in the degree of success and so-called 'good luck' we encounter. We all subconsciously know what we deserve, based on our past actions and intentions. There are usually at least two ways of interpreting most events, and the subconscious mind is the chief governor of how we interpret each event—whether we see it as positive or negative; good luck or bad. So one of the most important secrets in attracting good fortune is to make sure the subconscious is working in our favor. We can do that by living in line with our fundamental higher values which are also the universal interests of the human race.

The more you can configure your life so that you are working in harmony with universal interests, the more you will be able to gain from life—and indeed from this book. However, no book-knowledge can be as powerful as the forces within your own mind, governing the degree that the universe is working with you or against you. Until you can take this on board, the rest of the book can be of little immediate benefit.

❖ *I find that the harder I work, the more luck I seem to have.*
   —Thomas Jefferson

Many of us can relate to the above quote, but notice that it only applies when our efforts are in line with the true interests of the human race, i.e., in harmony with Higher Law rather than lower, purely selfish desires. Once your actions, pursuits and intentions are on the side of Higher Law, everything changes: Now, the harder you work (within reason), the luckier you become. Similarly, the more courageous you are (within reason), the luckier you become. Once Higher Law is firmly your ally, you have a magical combination key for attracting good fortune: it is the combination of **effort** and **courage**. Without concord with Higher Law, these two completely lose potency as attractors of good fortune.

❖ *Luck favors the bold.—Virgil*

Let's get three great allies on our side!

Paying heed to our inner voice of conscience is a step towards higher intelligence, or wisdom, which is perhaps the most powerful asset we can develop when it comes to achieving lasting success, personal fulfillment and inner peace.

So right from the start, let us first of all gain the allegiance of our three greatest supporters:

    1) Our own higher intelligence,
    2) Our subconscious mind
    3) The human race

The amazing power of beginner's luck

The first time I ever threw a dart at a dartboard, the dart landed in the center of the bull's eye. The first time I bought a set of raffle tickets, I won prize after prize with the few tickets I had. The first time I ever took part in a quiz, I won. The first time I entered a painting competition, I won. You may be able to think of examples where beginner's luck has favored you. It happens often enough to suggest that beginner's luck is something more tenable than pure coincidence. So isn't this something we should seek to take advantage of?

How does beginner's luck occur?

There is much evidence to indicate that we all possess phenomenal abilities, but more often than not, we cannot access these abilities because we tell ourselves we can't. Whenever we fail at something, we reinforce, subconsciously, the idea that we are not clever enough or skillful enough to succeed at the pursuit in question. The more times we fail, the more this inner vote of no-confidence is reinforced.

When we try something for the very first time, we can often do very well, provided we don't have any preconceived ideas and assumptions that we can't do it, or that we don't have what it takes. We often find we do amazingly well, because we have not yet had the chance to program ourselves into believing we can't do it, or that success is beyond our reach.

Superhuman powers

There are many accounts of people with normal strength seemingly acquiring superhuman power in times of urgent need. There are several accounts of people who have managed to lift a car off a person trapped underneath and fighting for their life, long enough for them to be pulled out. The need to act was so imperative that they did not stop to consider the notion that they didn't have the strength to achieve such a feat.

Our own minds seem to be the limiting factor. There are recorded cases where people have incurred brain damage during an accident and have subsequently acquired amazing talents. Presumably it was that part of the brain responsible for the limiting ideas that became defunct due to injury.

In 2006 Derek Amato from Denver, Colorado suffered brain injury during an accident. Afterwards, he soon discovered he had acquired amazing dexterity as a pianist, a gift he had never before possessed. He soon became famous and secured a recording contract and endless requests for concert appearances worldwide. There are many other similar cases that have been documented around the world.

Beginner's luck and Shoshin

Lady Luck tends to reward beginner's courage. So if there is something you have always wanted to do but have not had the courage to try, due to assumptions that you don't have sufficient skill or experience, perhaps you should reconsider. If you take the plunge and give it your best, you may be amazed at how fortune favors you—especially if you adopt what the Japanese refer to as 'shoshin', which loosely translated, means 'beginner's mind'. You effectively tell the voice of doubt that whispers in your ear, to go and take long walk along a short pier, while you give the task your best shot!

Shoshin is widely taught in oriental martial arts schools. It is about having an attitude of openness, eagerness, and lack of preconceptions, similar to the approach of a complete beginner who has not yet convinced himself to believe he can't do well or that success is bound to be very difficult. It is recommended that one adopts shoshin, even when tackling challenges where one already (theoretically) has the training and skills to do well. Along with having courage, this is one way we open the channels for 'beginner's luck'—even when we are not a beginner!

Commitment and positive action invites good fortune

People talk about the so-called Law of Attraction, but this book subscribes to an entirely more effective law; not the Law of Attraction so much as the Law of <u>Action</u>!

Positive, well-chosen action almost always brings positive results. It also lifts your mood and thus your energy enthusiasm for further action and further progress. Keep this cycle going to crank into life an engine of positive progress that will change everything for you! The hardest part is often simply goading yourself into getting up and making that first turn of the crank handle—but that's actually easy. Every great enterprise begins with a single small step, and by taking one step at a time, tremendous things can be accomplished with ease!

This book urges you to invite good fortune and real change, by committing to your exciting dreams and ambitions by taking courageous but judicious positive action towards their accomplishment. It's simple but powerful magic!

RECOMMENDED ACTION STEPS

1) You can only take advantage of good luck unless you notice and acknowledge it! Every day, write down at least six fortunate things that occur during the day. Adopting this habit makes you increasingly 'luck-aware'. You will become increasingly happy and fortunate, as you take fuller advantage of the good fortune that occurs each day.

2) Make a list of things you would like to have done, but didn't, because you feared you didn't have the necessary abilities. Consider what we have explored, regarding beginner's luck; you may be inclined to pluck up the courage to have a go. Consider also Virgil's words: 'Luck favours the bold.' You may be surprised how well you do!

3) Reflect on all the activities you engage in. Do any of them contravene the Higher Law we have discussed? See if you can change or eliminate such activities, or modify them, to harmonize with Higher Law. The long-term benefits for you and all who you come in contact with will be far-reaching. And the whole world will be your friend!

4) Keep watch over your thoughts. Are they always in harmony with Higher Law, or do you sometimes harbour thoughts of harm, revenge, spite, malice, etc? Through vigilance, it becomes easier to nip such thoughts in the bud before they become habit. Such thoughts tend to be repeated, thus becoming habits and attitudes that lead you into trouble of one kind or another, sooner or later.

5) Reflect occasionally on the times when you have defied selfish inclinations in order to act in harmony with Higher Law. It pays to remind your subconscious mind of such merits and the underlying goodness within you that prompted them. The chances are it will reward you in unexpected ways - ways that seem like pure good luck!

LOA vs. GFA
Debunking the 'Law of Attraction'

❖ *The general root of superstition [is that] men observe when things hit, and not when they miss, and commit to memory the one, and pass over the other.* —Sir Francis Bacon

We should be careful what we believe — especially when seeking shortcuts to personal success and fulfillment. The world is littered with alluring beliefs, superstitions, and deceptive get-rich-quick schemes. Many of these have become big businesses for the promoters. They advocated the scheme so convincingly that hoards of people are conned. And oftentimes, when they begin to see reality under the light of healthy objective scrutiny, they can often be easily goaded 'back on track' with a fresh dose of conditioning from the skilful promoters who need to keep the belief alive in order to bring food to their table.

This book shuns superstition and faulty logic, focusing only on proven methods that really work, in almost all circumstances!

Many self-help books tout the so-called 'law of attraction' as the ultimate secret of personal success. Fortunes have been spent on slick marketing to persuade potential book-buyers of the theorem's validity. Millions of wishful thinkers have swallowed this would-be 'magic pill' that promises to solve all problems for everyone! Such books typically promise that you can infallibly 'manifest' material wealth and abundance without even having to work for it.

If this were true, everyone who bought into the doctrine should now be millionaires, because, all they would need to do is buy a lottery ticket and 'manifest' a big win! Clearly, this is not the case. The only thing missing from this supposed panacea for all problems was an honest dose of reality. This so-called 'law' of attraction, just doesn't stand up to scrutiny, as millions of aspirants have discovered, though many prefer to live in denial, because to entertain scepticism would be 'negative', thus contravening the whole philosophy!

The alleged 'law' of attraction is largely a confidence trick!

The disappointing fact is that this alleged Law of Attraction, (LOA), is not a law at all; it is mostly wishful thinking. It doesn't require rocket-science to expose the fallacy of the belief that our reality is entirely manifested by what we think and believe. Everyone who lives in the real world should be able to remember numerous occasions in their lives when they have anticipated something bad happening, only to be greatly relieved when it failed to occur. They will also remember occasions when they have expected something wonderful would happen - but were disappointed when it didn't.

This doctrine holds that thought creates reality and that we create our reality by what we believe and imagine. It claims that we always attract what we envisage and expect. (It's a 'law', they claim!)

If this were true, the Titanic would not have sunk! Think about it; everyone believed that ship was unsinkable! And no-one would ever walk into a plate glass door and hurt themselves! They didn't notice the glass door in front of them so how could they have mentally manifested the accident? People who imagine that the ground they walk on is safe would never slip on a banana skin or stub their toe on a proud paving stone! So clearly, this supposed 'law' is not really a law. Countless examples of the LOA failing to deliver occur every minute of every day, yet adherents to the doctrine conveniently overlook this, and prefer to live in denial.

One of the fundamental axioms of worldly success should surely be to be grounded in truth and objective common sense, and not to count on superstition to bring about the good fortune. What is superstition? A superstition is a falsehood that people have been conditioned, brainwashed or programmed to accept as truth. The LOA, as popularly understood, is a case in point!

The LOA, as expounded in the book *The Secret* and earlier books on which it was based, does have some tentative (but only tentative) basis in fact. That's why it occasionally seems to work (although not due to any magical metaphysical concept such as 'attracting' or 'manifesting').

Two plus two does not equal five!

The LOA is a popular delusion that was arrived at by observing some genuine cause-and-effect phenomena, and arriving at a wild and exaggerated conclusion: that our thoughts create our reality, without exception. (If there was an exception, it wouldn't be a so-called 'law', would it?) However, this philosophy stands up to neither empirical nor rational scrutiny.

The Secret is based on a philosophy expounded in a much earlier book called The Master Key, written by Charles F Haanel. It is a philosophy based on the observation that thinking in a certain way tends to result in good outcomes. The Master Key was written, over a century ago, when cognitive psychology, behavioral neuroscience and sound logic were not as developed and well researched as they are today. Back in 1912, the only explanation offered, explaining the observation that positive visualisation produced positive results was a metaphysical one. There was no other available way to rationalise it. In a similar way, the Native Americans used to bury a fish head in the same hole where they planted corn. They observed the positive effects on plant growth and assumed it was due to magical or spiritual effects. Of course, the effects were really due to the nutrients provided by the decomposing fish. Magic invariably gets debunked sooner or later, often due to developments in scientific understanding.

What about quantum physics?

Quantum physics recently proved that matter is subject to the affects of human observation, they tell us. However, any such effects have only been observed on a subatomic level. Many claims of psychokinesis and manifestation without physical intervention on a macrocosmic level occur, but no such effect has ever been reliably reproduced under controlled conditions to date.

The reason why *The Secret* was such a best-seller is mainly due to the persuasive skills of its authors and the sophistication of the marketing. Most people are more likely to believe a claim if it is even slightly convincingly promising. It is human nature to clutch at straws and give the straw the benefit of any doubt.

Wouldn't it be wonderful if it were really true that achieving anything substantial didn't require work – if all we need to do is imagine it and hey-presto, 'the universe' supplies it!

However, before we consign the LOA to the trash can, it will pay us to see if we can salvage any useful components from it. Although the LOA is clearly a castle made of sand, it is built on some useful foundation stones that we can salvage and benefit from. So let's sift the useful wheat from the bogus chaff, and thresh out the good from the bad and the ugly!

The Good

Positive thinking and imagining good outcomes are two genuinely useful foundation stones underlying the LOA. These can genuinely benefit us, sometimes in seemingly miraculous ways. Read on to understand why.

It has been calculated that every second, our senses are bombarded with around 40 million bits of information. However, our brains can only process about one millionth of this amount. The subconscious mental faculty that decides which millionth part of that colossal load our brains should bother to process, is called the *sensory gating system* (SGS for short). It chooses what to register and process, based on how the subconscious mind has been conditioned and programmed. If the subconscious mind has been programmed to believe that negative outcomes are important, due to repeated visualizations to that effect, the RLS will mainly notice incoming information that is pertinent to these negative outcomes that have been imprinted on the subconscious mind. Conversely, if the subconscious mind has been programmed to believe that a positive outcome is important, it will tend to notice incoming information helpful to the realization of the positive outcome. If programmed to bring about good outcomes the RLS really can sift out some remarkably fortunate finds among the colossal influx of information that passes through its filter. And the result can often seem like amazingly good luck. To the unenlightened, this can look like magic and it is what gave rise to the rise to the exaggerated claims of the 'LOA'.

Positive thinking is the useful 'wheat' we can put to good use. Positive thinking and a positive mental attitude really do help to bring about positive outcomes. If we are preoccupied with imagining negative outcomes, we are diverting attention that could be better used, helping to bring about positive outcomes. Infusing your goals and ambitions with positive, realistic beliefs and thoughts has a direct effect on feelings and mood, which in turn affects behavior and performance. So thinking positively does tend to produce positive results. There is no magic or metaphysics in this. We are not attracting circumstances through our 'vibration' or programming 'the universe' to deliver what we want!

The Bad

A young lady is introduced to a focus group centred on the LOA. She swallows the seductive bait, hook, line and sinker. As she is struggling to make ends meet, she decides to buy scratch-card lottery tickets while applying LOA technique of visualising a big win with positive intention. She buys ticket after ticket and eventually she wins something. There is no metaphysical law at play here; just the everyday law of probability. Then, as coincidence or probability would have it, she wins another small amount. "Ah!", she thinks, "This Law of Attraction really works!" She eagerly proceeds to 'enlighten' her friends and relatives. However, one straight-thinking friend comments: "I don't want to rain on your parade, but your small wins were completely consistent with normal odds, and not miraculous at all." After that comment, and in keeping with the laws of probability, she experiences no further immediate wins. Rather than accept reality, she now blames her concerned friend for her subsequent lack of wins! She blames him for infecting her with the vibrations of negativity and scepticism, thus killing her winning streak!

❖ *Every occult practitioner can come up with one good story about a lucky hit. Some of these stories are astonishing indeed. ...but hold tight to your scepticism and your money.*
—Max Gunther

❖ *The general root of superstition [is that] men observe when things hit, and not when they miss, and commit to memory the one, and pass over the other.* —Sir Francis Bacon

The Ugly

If you have a friend who subscribes to this distorted doctrine, you may have noticed that if you stumble on any kind of misfortune, you are unlikely to get much support or sympathy from them, because they do not want to be infected by your 'vibrations' of 'negativity'. To provide any sympathy or compassion would be to reward the negative thinking that they believe caused your misfortune! They believe that all misfortune is the fault of the sufferer, and nothing happens by chance. Compassion is illogical in this ideology. On the contrary, it makes sense to the LOA faithful to deride unfortunates for their own 'self-inflicted' circumstances!

Belief in the LOA can even be downright dangerous. Recently, a real-life woman went on a backpacking tour of Africa. She chose to believe in the power of LOA-style positive imagination to protect her from disease during her travels, and so opted out of the advised inoculations prior to her trip.

That decision proved fatal. She caught a lethal form of cerebral malaria and died as a result. Thousands of other examples of the failure of the LOA to work as promised could be cited here, but I am sure you get the point.

Nevertheless, the occasional apparent efficacy of the doctrine is enough to keep the LOA's hopeful proponents sold on the wild claims that any outcome one wishes for can be manifested by thought! To think anything else would be 'negative' and bound to ensure failure! Can you see the self-perpetuating, bogus, circular logic here?

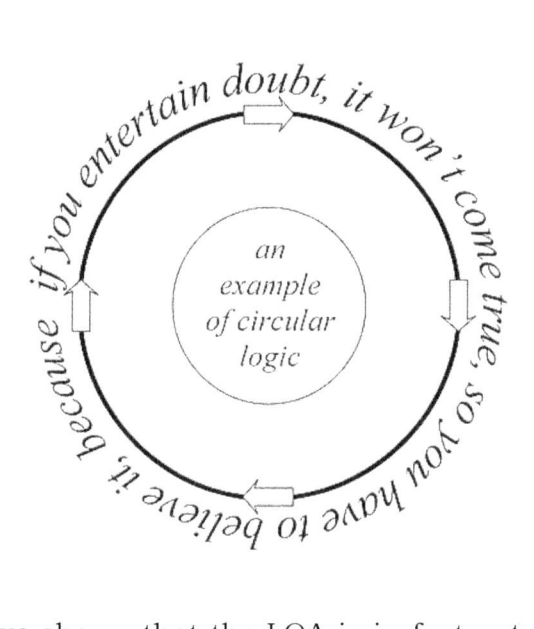

an example of circular logic

entertain doubt, it won't come true, so you have to believe it, because if you

We have shown that the LOA is in fact not a law at all. Goal-focused action, on the other hand, always produces results so is far more deserving of being labelled a 'law'. Goal-focused ACTION in particular, is the most reliable way to improve one's fortune. If we practice GFA instead of relying on the LOA, we will do much better, in the long run. It almost always results in satisfaction rather than disappointment. This book is primarily about GFA. It doesn't deny that imagination and positive intention are useful tools, but it does not attempt to delude anyone with promises of easily acquired riches, manifested by the mere application of imagination without action. If you put your faith in imagination alone, you will probably have a long wait before your dreams come true, as if by magic – if indeed they come true at all. So why wait? Why not take concerted goal-focused ACTION to bring about what you want, while applying positive thinking to make the process more effective? Positive action begets positive thinking and positive thinking begets positive action. This happy upward spiral brings results – but not due to mystical, metaphysical force, 'vibration' or 'cosmic ordering' directed at 'the Universe'.

Whether or not you choose to subscribe to the 'Law of Attraction', this book can be of immense value to you, because it shares alternative concepts that really work!

❖ *Superstition is the religion of feeble minds.* — Edmund Burke

RECOMMENDED ACTION STEP

Time for some deep reflection and introspection! Consider carefully whether you have any tendency to be influenced by superstitious ideologies, such as astrology, numerology, the tarot, what a fortune teller once told you or whether a black cat crossed your path recently. If so, determine to adopt a more grounded, objective position, taking responsibility for your fortunes and taking positive, targeted action towards achieving what you want from life.

3
YOUR INNERMOST DREAMS
GIVE THEM DUE CONSIDERATION!

❖ *As soon as you start to pursue a dream, your life wakes up and everything has meaning.—Barbara Sher*

To maximize our potential for true happiness, it pays to identify our deepest heartfelt wishes and dreams. This is not always easy if we have at some point, buried them or consigned them to the bin labeled 'unachievable'. It can often pay to revive those neglected dreams occasionally, and reconsider whether they are as unachievable as we may have surmised. This chapter helps you uncover and re-examine those dreams that you may have allowed to fade into obscurity. They are a vital part of who you are, and what you might become. They can be a source of vital energy and motivation, and a potential path to enviable self-fulfillment.

Have you heard of people being buried alive? This dreadful occurrence was quite common before medical methods were reliably able to indentify true death as opposed to coma or catalepsy. This horror happened to the mother of Robert E. Lee, the famous American Civil War general. Fortunately, a servant of the Lee household heard noises coming from the grave. The coffin was exhumed and the woman was found alive! She fully recovered and later gave birth to a son who would become the South's famous general.

Many have not been so fortunate. Coffins have been exhumed and evidence has been found indicating that the supposedly deceased had woken up after burial and had fought desperately to escape from their terrible predicament.

Thankfully, such mistakes are rarely made nowadays, at least with regard to the physical aspect of a person. But how many times have precious, heartfelt dreams been buried while still capable of being nurtured to full, glorious fruition? Many wonderful dreams are aborted and buried without being given a chance. Have you perhaps done this yourself? It is surely worth re-examining our deepest unfulfilled dreams to consider whether they can be revived and nurtured to our profound benefit. Using the guidance in this book, you may well be able to achieve those dreams after all, and with much less difficulty than you previously assumed.

Many people reach old age in a tragic state of grief because they failed to pursue their most treasured and passionate dreams. Now you don't have to be one of them!

Cultivate your dreams!

Everybody has a dream of some kind. It may be a longing for something—possibly without any conviction that it could ever come true. Dreams are what make us feel unique. They can give us that spark of hope that can mitigate the trials and tribulations of the workaday world.

Most of us were taught at an early age, for better or for worse, that some things you just have to do without—that dreams are unrealistic flights of fancy that we should let go of for our own good. Most people eventually lose touch with their dreams, or train themselves to close their minds to them, or convince themselves that dreams are a dangerous illusion, not to be believed in. This is a shame, because most dreams can be made reality, with enough faith and confidence. The very fact that you have a dream means that some part of you believes it could come true. That part is usually right. All that is needed is a little training in how to achieve it. This book will show you how to achieve dreams that seem almost unattainable.

If you can open up your awareness and tune in to your dreams, you will have found a powerful motivating force which can propel you to great heights of achievement and the consequent feelings of self-worth. We may have learned to shut them out, but our dreams are always there with us, in an obscure corner of our mind. In moments of quiet reflection we occasionally get fleeting glimpses of that inner dream that would spell true paradise for us, if it could only come true. These glimpses are often triggered by beautiful sights, certain music, or people's personalities. Look out for those glimpses. Contemplate them and build on them.

Dreams have a formidable underlying power. They generate a power that sustains us and gives us vitality and hope. To possess a dream is to be able to rise above the trials and tribulations of the material world at will.

Your dreams may be easier to achieve than you thought

When you are once again in touch with your dreams, consider that it might just be possible to achieve them. Perhaps all you need is a bit more courage, and a bit more confidence. By learning the techniques outlined in this book, you will have far greater power to make those dreams become reality. You will gain the confidence necessary to be a new kind of winner.

Once you have a better idea of your dreams and governing values, and what sort of person you want to become, you will be in a powerful position to define some daring personal goals that will mobilize your entire being and awaken your latent powers.

Goals alone often lack real motivating power, but you can supercharge yours by orienting them towards the realization of your ultimate dreams. The great icons of world history were merely people who had dreams—and believed in their ability to achieve them—and had the courage to try. Whether or not you desire personal fame, you can triumph to no lesser degree, and soar to great heights of satisfaction and self-esteem.

Specify exactly why it would benefit you to achieve your dreams

Define one or more compelling reasons why it will benefit you to achieve your dreams. Write it down in your A-Log. What you write will be the central impetus that will keep you going even when discouraging events make progress challenging.

- *Dreams are extremely important. You can't do it unless you imagine it. —George Lucas*

- *Too many of us are not living our dreams because we are living our fears. —Les Brown*

- *Think big and don't listen to people who tell you it can't be done. Life's too short to think small. —Tim Ferriss*

- *We may place blame, give reasons, and even have excuses; but in the end, it is an act of cowardice to not follow your dreams. —Steve Maraboli*

- *Dreaming, after all, is a form of planning. —Gloria Steinem*

- *The dreamers are the saviors of the world. —James Allen*

- *Miracles start to happen when you give as much energy to your dreams as you do to your fears. —Richard Wilkins*

RECOMMENDED ACTION STEPS

1) Dare to imagine what it would be like to actually achieve your dreams. Think big and aim high, because this book reveals many tools and techniques that can literally multiply your powers to achieve and succeed!

2) Write down your wildest dreams — and your not-so-wild ones! If your inclination to indulge in wild dreams has been quelled somewhere along your path, revive it now! In your A-Log, start listing your dreams. This important practice will help you realize the direction your life could take and help you choose the best goals to set with a view to your ultimate fulfillment.

3) Define one or more compelling reasons why it would benefit you to achieve each of your dreams. What you write about this will provide the central impetus that will keep you going even when discouraging events occur.

4) Be sure to put these things in writing. This forces you to clarify exactly what your ideals and dreams are. This greatly helps the conscious and subconscious part of your mind to set in motion powerful forces to help you achieve your wishes. The other reason is that we want to be able to refer back to them. That's part of the process.

5) Remember: It is generally better to keep your A-Log totally private - for your eyes only! That way it will have far more power than otherwise. If you share your ideas and plans with someone, that person may subtly sabotage your ideas, even without intending to.

4
THE PERSON YOU'LL BECOME
DEVELOPING THE CHARACTER

❖ *Parents can only give good advice or put them on the right path, the final forming of a person's character lies in their own hands.* —Anne Frank

The cornerstone of significant self-improvement is our own inner character. Depending on our characteristics, our progress will be either easy and enjoyable, or sporadic and difficult. So this chapter looks at the all-important subject of adopting the best personal characteristics before spending too much time on circumstantial gains.

If a building is to last, it needs a good foundation. The same applies when building a successful future. The foundation of your successful future will be your personality. The next important action you are about to take is to write down a description of the person you want to become.

The person you'd like to become

In your A-Log, you will be asked to describe the person you want to become. Write in the first person, in the present tense. In other words, instead of writing: "I will be friendly and approachable", write: *"I am becoming increasingly friendly and approachable."* At first, write quickly and freely, listing all the traits you can think of. Don't worry about being inaccurate or unsure of yourself; you can go back later and change what you have written as many times as necessary, until you are satisfied. However, as people constantly change, you may find that this situation never arrives. As you write, you may think of more things to add to your notes.

Your personal code of living

In your A-Log, define your *personal code of living*, including your fundamental governing values. This is important, because your governing values are your foundations of success and fulfillment. The time you take over these will be time well spent. By defining your governing values first, you will be in a position to then define worthwhile goals that are worth committing to. Only working towards goals that reflect your governing values will result in inner peace and fulfillment. Goals that are in harmony with your deepest governing values are easier to achieve; because your subconscious mind will be your willing ally.

Defining the traits you want

Imagine you are attending your own funeral. Listen to the speeches your friends are making about you. Are you satisfied with what they say? If not, what would you really like to hear? This should give you clues about your desired traits. There follows a list of character traits. Tick off any that inspire you or provoke a positive emotional response. Then for each one selected, write an affirmation that explains why that word will describe the new you. For example, with the trait 'educated', one person wrote: "I am educated; I educate myself every time I notice deficiencies in my knowledge."

Every day, spend some time behaving like the new you that you have described. This way you will slowly but surely transform yourself. Here is a long list of qualities that you might wish to draw upon.

able	calm	daring	empathetic
adaptable	carefree	decent	enchanting
affable	caring	dependable	enduring
affectionate	centered	determined	energetic
altruistic	charismatic	dexterous	engaging
amiable	charitable	different	enlightened
amazing	charming	diligent	enterprising
amusing	cheerful	diplomatic	entertaining
artistic	compassionate	discerning	enthusiastic
assertive	confident	disciplined	entrepreneurial
astute	congenial	dramatic	erudite
balanced	constructive	dynamic	exemplary
benevolent	creative	educated	extraordinary
brave	cultured	efficient	fair
brilliant	cunning	eloquent	faithful

fearless	imaginative	mighty	polite
fit	important	mirthful	positive
fluent	incredible	moral	postured
focused	independent	motivated	powerful
forgiving	indispensable	natural	productive
free	industrious	neat	professional
friendly	informed	neighborly	profound
fulfilled	ingenious	noble	progressive
fun	inspired	nurturing	prolific
gallant	inspirational	open-minded	prosperous
generous	intelligent	optimistic	proud
gentle	invaluable	organized	prudent
genuine	inventive	outstanding	pure-hearted
good	joyful	parental	purposeful
graceful	kind	participating	radiant
gracious	leading	passionate	rational
great	learned	patient	ready
gregarious	liberal	peaceful	reasonable
handy	liberated	perceptive	receptive
happy	literate	persevering	relaxed
healthy	loveable	personable	reliable
helpful	loving	persuasive	resilient
heroic	lovely	philosophical	resolute
honest	magnanimous	physical	resourceful
honorable	magnetic	pioneering	respectable
hopeful	magnificent	playful	responsible
hospitable	masterful	pleasant	responsive
humane	mature	poetic	robust
humble	merciful	poised	romantic
humorous	merry	polished	sensitive

sensuous	sublime	transcendental	virtuous
serene	subtle	triumphant	visionary
sexy	successful	true	vivacious
sharp	supportive	trustworthy	vivid
sharing	supreme	truthful	warm
significant	sweet	unafraid	wealthy
sincere	sympathetic	unbiased	well-balanced
single-minded	tactful	understanding	well-read
skilful	talented	unique	well-wishing
sociable	tenacious	unpredictable	willing
soulful	thoughtful	unusual	wise
special	thrifty	valiant	with it
spectacular	thriving	valued	witty
spiritual	tidy	versatile	wonderful
spontaneous	timeless	vibrant	worthy
sportive	tolerant	vigilant	young-at-heart
strong	tough	vigorous	zany
studious	tranquil	virile	zealous

❖ *If you want a quality, act as if you already had it.*
  —William James

❖ *To be yourself in a world that is constantly trying to make you something else is the greatest accomplishment.*
  —Ralph Waldo Emerson

❖ *Men of genius are admired, men of wealth are envied, men of power are feared; but only men of character are trusted.*
  —Proverb

❖ *Honor is the reward of virtue.* —Marcus Tulius Cicero

RECOMMENDED ACTION STEPS

1) Define your Personal Code of Living, including your fundamental governing values, in your A-Log. Review it regularly and refine it as necessary.

2) In your A-Log, describe the person you'd like to become. Review this regularly when you review your goals. Modify as necessary.

3) Spend some time every day, behaving according to the traits you have described. At the end of every day, write down, in your diary or A-Log, what you did and how you behaved to comply with this. Don't let yourself off the hook; do it every day!

5
THE IMPORTANCE OF GOALS
THE LINCHPIN OF ACHIEVEMENT

❖ *A goal without a plan is just a wish.*
   —Antoine de Saint-Exupéry

People who have goals succeed. People who don't have goals fail! The most outstanding feats of human accomplishment were made possible due to definite goals. By formulating a clear goal and orienting yourself towards it, you acquire a multiplied power to succeed. This simple action spells the difference between success and failure in all fields of human endeavour. In this chapter we focus on defining goals.

Being successful is simply a matter of deciding what you want, then taking the necessary steps to achieve it. Many people don't achieve goals because they simply don't set them in the first place. Many more fail because they simply don't believe they can succeed. You can build up your confidence in your ability to achieve your goals by imagining yourself achieving them. Use your imagination to experience the thrill you will enjoy if you achieve your dreams. Imagine vividly all the perils of NOT achieving your goals. Get worried! Use 'the stick' as well as 'the carrot' to goad yourself into action.

Your goals must reflect your governing values

Some people fail to achieve their goals because they lack motivation. This is often because their goals conflict with their fundamental beliefs and values. Therefore, before you start goal-setting, it is important to articulate your Personal Code of Living. If your goals contradict your deepest convictions and governing values, achieving them will be an uphill battle. To achieve goals quickly and easily, you need your heart and soul to be working *with* you; not against you! When you work towards goals that reflect your governing values, you'll experience inner peace and satisfaction.

Your goals must be in harmony with one another

Your goals should not conflict with one another. If the wheels on your car were pointing in different directions, you wouldn't make very swift progress, would you? The same applies to your goals. Many people fail because they are not wise to this. For example, a man has a goal to go into business for himself. He has another goal to improve his marriage. Unfortunately, his wife is unhappy because he doesn't spend much time with her. The two goals conflict; the particular business he is planning will demand that he spends even less time with his wife. Perhaps he should rethink his goals, and plan a business which can involve his wife, or manage from home.

Someone else wanted to spend more time on his hobby while saving more money. The two goals conflicted because his hobby demanded an investment of both money and time

Consider how changing your success rate in one area of your life could affect other areas. For example, how will your close relatives and loved ones react? How will that affect you? It's called 'systems thinking'.

Your goals should be primarily yours

When formulating a goal, ask yourself if it is your own personal goal, rather than something someone else has decided would be good for you! It's easier to achieve goals that come from your heart and help liberate the real you. Self-respect is the reward of a goal achieved, and that is usually more important than winning the respect of others. After all, you have to live with yourself every minute for the rest of your life; no one else does. Other people may come and go, but you'll always have yourself as company. Every personal victory of an achieved goal is a gem that will permanently enrich your life. One day, when you are old and dying, those gems will still be just as valuable to you.

Your goals benefit from being daring

Why bother with easy goals that promise mediocre rewards? Be daring and aim high! After all, you do not have to expect to achieve all your goals by the end of this week, or even this year. Don't succumb to the cowardly idea that you can't succeed. Every one of us has powers that are little short of miraculous. Much of our power lies dormant, but if we can awaken it, there is almost no limit to what we might achieve.

Take risks! People who don't, lead a humdrum existence. Try not to fear the unknown. Each one of us is nothing less than a genius in essence; however most of us have become handicapped by accepting negative suggestions from other people about our ability. You can achieve almost impossible goals if you simply take things a step at a time.

Your goals benefit from being exciting

Your goals will be easier and more enjoyable to attain if they excite you deeply. Charge yourself up by imagining the thrills and benefits of achieving them. The more intense the emotions you can evoke, the better. Cultivate a burning desire to succeed. Merely aiming at the same kind of uninspiring goals that most people aspire to will not evoke the kind of passion and excitement that is the magic ingredient for rapid success.

Your goals should be achievable

There's a fine line between goals that are daring and exciting, and goals that are downright impossible. A woman with no arms would be unwise set out to become a world-class boxing champion. A blind man would probably be unwise to set out to win the Grand Prix. Remember however, that many people have attained incredible success in spite of severe handicaps. People who have lost the use of one or more of their faculties tend to develop others to compensate.

Your goals should be clearly defined

The more specific you can be about the finer details of your goals, the better. The subconscious mind will often help you in surprising ways, if you feed it with clear specifics. Visualize your goals with as much clarity as you can. If it's a new house you're after, get a clear picture of all the details, including the kind of roof tiles, the color of the paintwork, the layout of the interior, the views from the windows and the neighbors. Every night as you lie in bed, picture the things and situations you want to achieve, clarifying any aspect of them that isn't clear. One important detail you should always include is the actual date of the goal's accomplishment! Always be sure to define that!

Then, mentally map out and visualize the steps you will take to achieve each goal. Visualizing the steps you'll take to achieve a goal is more important than visualizing the outcome. If you merely imagine enjoying the achieved goal, you may kid your subconscious mind that you have already achieved it and that there is therefore no point in making further effort! Most self-help books fail to point this out.

It's best to keep your goals secret

It's best to keep your goals to yourself, so keep your goal definitions in a private place, where no one will read them. Your goals are very personal, so if you must reveal them to anyone, make sure it's someone you trust and whose goals are in harmony with your own. In many cases, giving in to the temptation to discuss your goals with others will undermine your faith in your natural ability to succeed and may lay you open to ridicule, should you decide to change or modify your goals. You'll also be inviting subtle sabotage from people who, for one reason or another, prefer you not to succeed. It's sometimes a mistake to assume your close friends or relatives wish you to succeed.

❖ *A new idea is delicate. It can be killed by a sneer or a yawn; it can be stabbed to death by a quip and worried to death by a frown on the right man's brow.* —Charles Brower

Set goals in key areas of your life

There's much to be said for a holistic approach to self-improvement. It can cause problems for you if you become too passionately obsessed with attainment in just one area of life, while neglecting others. Why not set goals in all the main areas? Take a critical look at each area below. How do you feel about it? Consider the scope for personal improvement in each area:

- your career/business
- your social life
- your material assets
- your knowledge
- your physical self
- your mental self
- your leisure life
- your spiritual side

You may be able to think of additional key areas of your life in which to set goals. That is absolutely fine!

Now write down some things that it would benefit you to achieve or accomplish in each of these areas. Even if you aren't sure what your goals should be, it's a good idea to get something down on paper. This will give you a basis from which to develop a clearer picture. Take a critical look at the various aspects of your life. Forget any fear of change or lack of confidence in your abilities; simply look at the way things are, and the way you'd like them to be if you could have anything you desire. Tackle each area in turn, and in detail. When you get a glimpse of how you'd like things to be, write it down.

There follows some example goals that people have defined in each of eight key life areas. Naturally, yours will probably be entirely different, matching your own individual wants and needs. However, the following examples may trigger some ideas pertinent to your own dreams and objectives.

CAREER/BUSINESS

Own a successful business

Get a 30% raise before the end of the year

Get transferred to another branch

Become the market leader in my field

Get a job where I can develop my skills

Negotiate a higher salary

RELATIONSHIP/SOCIAL

Find my ideal partner

Get acquainted with inspiring people

Improve my marriage constantly

Take my partner or spouse out once a week

Befriend the neighbors

Rekindle old friendships

PHYSICAL DEVELOPMENT

Lose 25 lbs by next June

Jog at least 2 miles every day

Join a gym and attend work out three times a week

Become a karate black-belt

Be able to run for 1 hour, non-stop

LEISURE/HOBBY

Go on a world cruise

Take up rock climbing

Form a band

Go on a skiing holiday in the Alps

Learn to play the piano

Join an art class

LEARNING

Learn a foreign language

Learn to speed-read

Learn to type faster

Learn to drive

Get a degree

Learn to play a musical instrument

SPIRITUAL/ETHICAL

Become a vegetarian

Give 10% of my profits to charity

Do some voluntary work

Become 100% honest

Stop working for Crook & Sons

MENTAL

    Develop my sense of humor

    Develop my power of concentration

    Overcome my phobia

    Be more assertive

    Develop my willpower

    Become more optimistic and likeable

MATERIAL

    Buy a bigger house

    Buy the car I want

    Make a million dollars in 5 years

    Install a swimming pool

    Get a better computer

    Get satellite TV

    Get an extension built on the house

Devote time to developing your goals

By reviewing your goals daily (including the half-formed ones), you will start to clarify what your main goals should be. Look at each goal and ask yourself: "What do I hope to achieve by accomplishing this? What will be the real rewards?" and "What will be the penalty I'll pay if I fail to achieve this goal?" By asking these questions you may find there is another more important objective hidden behind it, or a hidden inner need that you could satisfy in an easier, or more direct way.

As you will be investing time, effort and possibly money in the pursuit of your goals, it makes sense to do some intensive thinking about what you really want to achieve. Commit yourself to spending at least half an hour each day for the next week or so, to this end. Every night at bedtime, review and refine your goals in your A-Log.

Build faith in your ability to succeed

Here's a technique that will boost your confidence in your ability to succeed like almost nothing else: For the next seven days exactly, stick to some chosen course of action. For example: cut out smoking, eat 1,000 calories a day, or spend half an hour a day on that project you never seem to have time for. Seven days is a nice easy chunk of time to cope with. Choose a course of action you know you can stick to, no matter what. Commit to it in your A-Log. When you succeed, your confidence in your ability to achieve your goals will soar—and so will your ability to achieve further goals.

Take some immediate step towards your goals!

This step is very important. It has tremendous power. Take some immediate action (even a small step) towards each of your goals, starting with the most exciting one.

Take a step towards your goals every day!

This step will take only a small amount of your time each day, but after several days of taking steps (even small ones) towards your goals, you will have set in motion an engine of accomplishment that has gained real momentum! After a week of these incremental daily steps, you will have made some real progress, and you will feel GREAT about that. Your confidence and self-esteem will enjoy a wonderful boost. Most people give up on their goals because they are daunted by the magnitude of the task. But by taking small but frequent steps, mountains can be moved with ease!

Always be goal-orientated

Why is it that some people seem to achieve much, while others achieve little? One of the main reasons is that high achievers are generally goal-oriented. They keep their goals in the forefront of their mind, and use them as the deciding factor every time they have a choice or a decision to make.

Your goals are your decision-gauge

If you were looking out for a bookcase to fit nicely in an alcove in your home, how would you go about it? The chances are, you'd look for a piece of string, cut it to the length of the alcove, and keep it in your pocket. Thus you have an effective gauge for measuring any bookcase you see when you are out shopping. It will quickly determine how well any bookcase you find will fit into your alcove. In exactly the same way, your goals are the yardsticks with which you should gauge the suitability of the many choices you make every day, seven days a week. When you are faced with a choice, simply ask yourself which one will best help you towards your goals. The more you do this, the more quickly you will achieve your goals, and the better you will feel about yourself inwardly.

Keep your goals in mind

If the bookcase hunter inadvertently left his piece of string at home, he'd be stumped as soon as found a bookcase that appealed to him. He'd either pass the bookcase by, or take a chance, and risk carrying home an item which might not fit. It's the same with your goals. Keep them with you as much as possible; in other words keep them in mind. Only by doing so, can you hope to make the best decisions and choices throughout each day.

Why do unsuccessful slimmers fail? Because they indulge in excess eating at moments when their slimming goal is not foremost in their minds. Why do nicotine quitters often fail? Because they allow their quitting-goal to fade from their minds, thus laying themselves open to old habits again. It's a simple formula that spells success. It applies to all forms of goal; not just those that involve giving up habits. Every time you let your goals fade from your mind, you are in a weak position; one where you could make a foolish decision or miss a valuable opportunity.

Keep your goals burning brightly

Your goals illuminate your path ahead so keep those beacons burning brightly! Keep kindling the desire, passion and determination you feel about your goals, and once burning, keep them well-fuelled. Feed those heart-warming fires with fresh firewood regularly. Talk to people who are enthused with similar goals. Study the things you want to achieve. Hone the skills you need to achieve them. Observe other people who are enjoying the things you want to achieve. Collect magazine cuttings, postcards, photographs, or any other relevant things that capture your imagination, and keep your passions alive and kicking.

- ❖ *Obstacles are those frightful things you see when you take your eyes off your goal. —Henry Ford*
- ❖ *The rung of a ladder was never meant to rest upon, but only to hold a man's foot long enough to enable him to put the other somewhat higher. —Thomas Henry Huxley*

- *Don't be afraid to take a big step if one is indicated; you can't cross a chasm in two small jumps. —David Lloyd George*

- *What you get by achieving your goals is not as important as what you become by achieving your goals. —Zig Ziglar*

- *Map out your future, but do it in pencil.*
  —Jon Bon Jovi

- *You must have long-range goals to keep you from being frustrated by short-range failures. —Charles C. Noble*

RECOMMENDED ACTION STEPS

1) In your A-Log, in a section allocated to defining goals, list some things you'd really like to achieve in some key areas of your life. Don't be afraid to aim high, but make sure they are goals that are worthy of commitment.

2) Take some immediate step towards each of your goals as soon as you have decided on them. Start with your most exciting goal. Do not omit this powerful step!

3) Every day, take at least one step (even a small one, but the bigger the better) towards each of your goals.

4) Be goal-oriented as from now, and make your everyday decisions based on how well they further you towards your main goals.

5) Each night, as you lie in bed, visualize the goals you aim to achieve, and the steps you must take to achieve them. And remember to consider the reasons why successfully achieving your goals will benefit you.

❖ *Held in the palms of thousands of disgruntled people over the centuries have been ideas worth millions – if they only had taken the first step and then followed through.*
—*Robert M. Hayes*

6
A SITUATION-TRANSFORMER
IMPROVE LIFE ON FOUR FRONTS

❖ *Man is a tool-using animal.... Nowhere do you find him without tools; without tools he is nothing, with tools he is all. —Thomas Carlyle*

In this chapter, we introduce a powerful tool to improve any situations in four different dimensions! We call it the Pyramid Plan Situation Transformer (PPST). It is particularly helpful for helping you define some key goals.

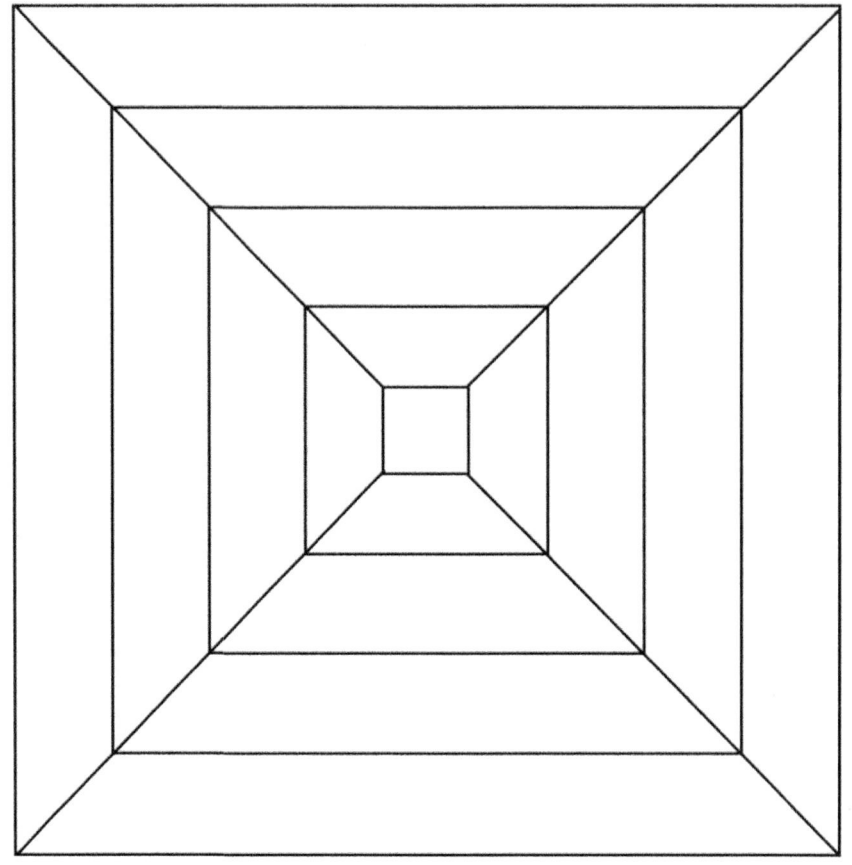

The Pyramid Plan Situation Transformer (PPST)

The Pyramid Plan Situation Transformer (PPST for short) is so called because it looks like the plan-view of a pyramid with its capstone removed. It is an amazingly effective tool for quickly making plans to improve your life in the most important areas. To use it, you simply copy the diagram onto a sheet of paper. (It doesn't have to be immaculately drawn!) You will then write in the blank spaces. It provides you with a bird's eye view of any complex subject, situation or problem that concerns you and gives you a way of defining appropriate improvements and solutions. It gets you from where you are to where you want to be, in a simple way with a clear overview. After you've tried it, you'll realize how useful it is. Use it to get a clear picture of how you can improve any situation that has a number of different aspects, departments or categories.

How to fill in your PPST

The central square always represents the subject you are working on. You could start by looking at your life situation. In the center, you'd write your name or "Me". Then in the four sections immediately outside the central square, write some brief titles representing important areas of your life such as **Health, Wealth, Social, Protection, Ethical, Spiritual**, etc.

Now in the sectors immediately outside these, briefly describe aspects of these areas that you're not 100% happy about. In the sections outside these, write how you would prefer each aspect of your situation to be.

Finally, in the outermost sections, write down what you resolve to do to bring about the desired improvements. If you find that each section of your PPST contains a particularly complicated subject, you could draw a separate PPST devoted to it alone. You can apply the PPST to any situation that needs sorting out or improving. Here is an example of one person's PPST, filled in:

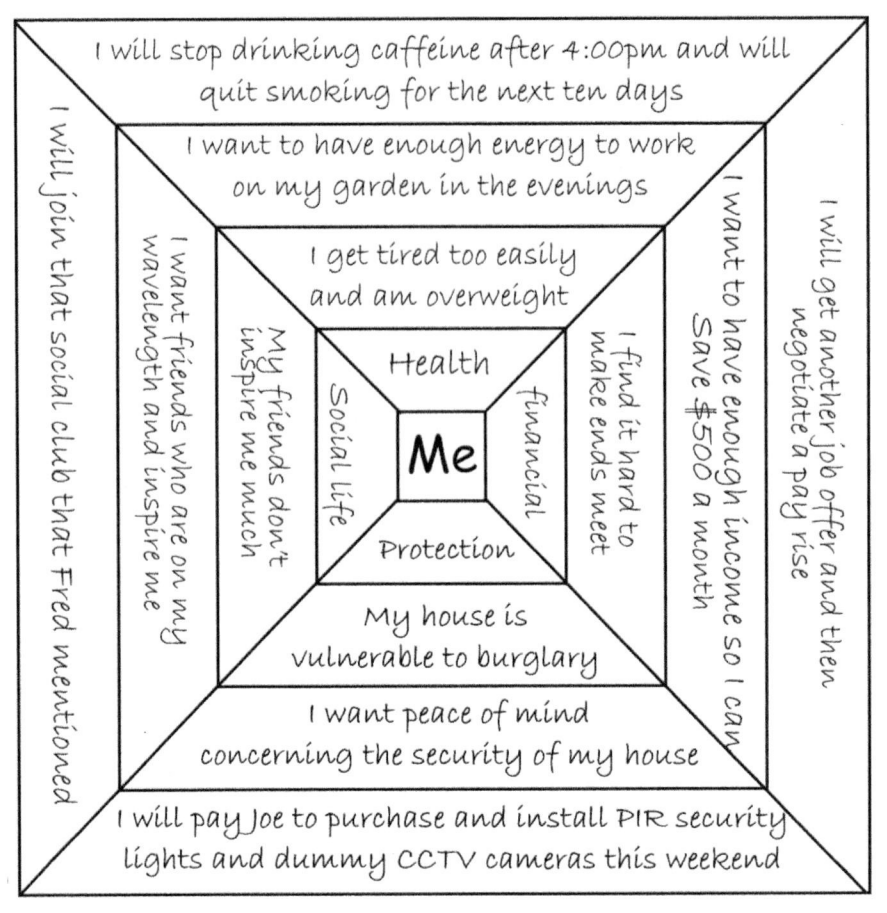

One person's PPST, planning improvements for his immediate future

Outer ring (action steps):
- I will stop drinking caffeine after 4:00pm and will quit smoking for the next ten days
- I will get another job offer and then negotiate a pay rise
- I will pay Joe to purchase and install PIR security lights and dummy CCTV cameras this weekend
- I will join that social club that Fred mentioned

Second ring (goals):
- I want to have enough energy to work on my garden in the evenings
- I want to have enough income so I can save $500 a month
- I want peace of mind concerning the security of my house
- I want friends who are on my wavelength and inspire me

Third ring (problems):
- I get tired too easily and am overweight
- I find it hard to make ends meet
- My house is vulnerable to burglary
- My friends don't inspire me much

Inner square (Me): Health, Financial, Protection, Social life

---

Blank, printable PPST charts can be obtained FREE, subject to availability, by visiting this book's website:
WWW.FFFBOOK.COM

A good approach to apply

Among the ancient metaphysical scriptures of India, there is reference to a system of categorization that can be applied with phenomenal suitability to the PPST. The system categorizes our worldly needs into four types, each of which require our attention if we are to live optimally. In Western terms, these equate to the four areas listed below. If you want a quick, broadly universal and all-encompassing quartet of quadrants to apply your PPST to, these could be it!

- *Matters concerning love and harmonious relations.*
- *Matters concerning material wealth and gain*
- *Matters concerning physical health*
- *Matters concerning protection*

Think of these four key areas of potential improvement as a good, off-the-cuff universal set of areas to think about when seeking to improve your situation.

In some situations, you may find it helpful to have more than four quadrants to map your improvements on. To this end, you can draw up a PPST with twice as many divisions as follows:

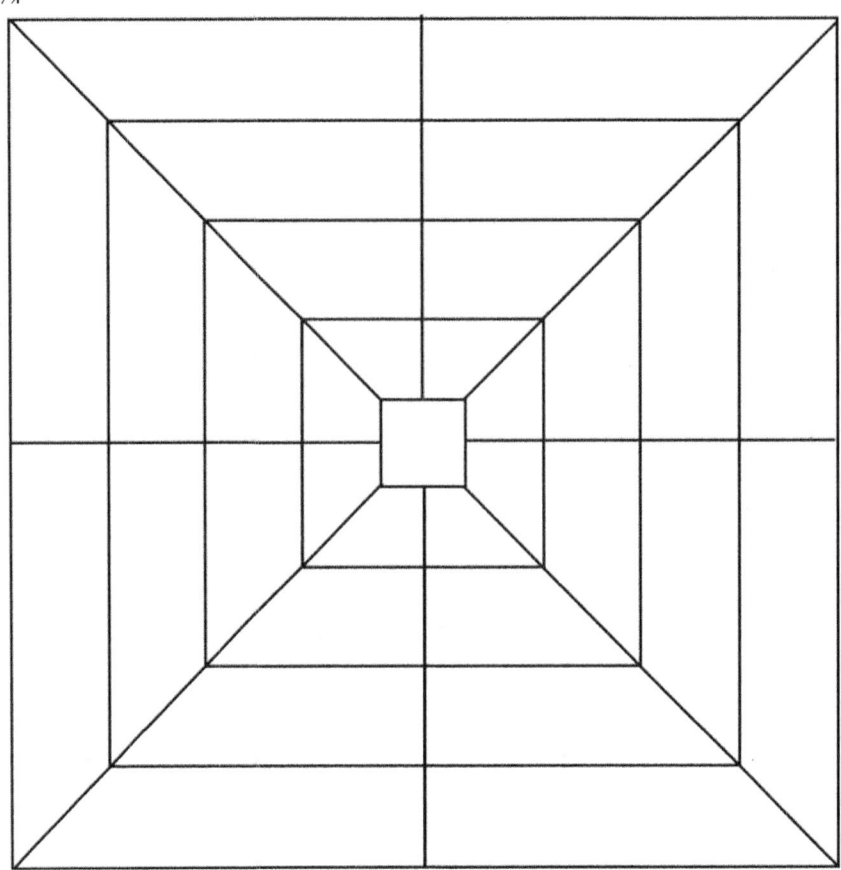

PPST with extra divisions

RECOMMENDED ACTION STEP

Draw a PPST for any situation that needs attention. Take a blank page in your A-Log. Draw four concentric squares as shown in the diagram and fill it in according to some situation of your own. Get into the habit of applying this excellent tool for improving your situations. Always write the central core of the issue in the center and work outwards.

7
EXAMINE YOUR HABITS
They Can Make or Break You

❖ *Your net worth to the world is usually determined by what remains after your bad habits are subtracted from your good ones.* —Benjamin Franklin

This chapter explores the all important subject of habits. As humans, we are creatures of habit and about half of everything we do is done by force of habit. Successful people are people with success-invoking habits, and failing people are those with self-defeating habits. We will learn a powerful technique for changing our habits.

You've heard it before: We are creatures of habit. There are some advantages to this; being a 'creature of habit' makes life much easier than it would otherwise be. Psychologists believe that about 40% of everything we do is done 'on autopilot', i.e., through the power of habit.

Take a simple car trip for example. We have done so much driving that we no longer need to pay much attention to how to change gear or use the turn signals; we just do it all subconsciously - so much so, that while driving, we can even carry out a conversation or plan the day's agenda. One woman was even caught applying her makeup while driving at 70mph. However, we don't recommend it – not least because she was pulled over and convicted of dangerous driving!

This ability to delegate complicated activities to the subconscious mind enables us to free up vast amounts of mental real estate for things that are of more immediate interest or more pressing importance.

Being a creature of habit also has some pitfalls. Unhelpful and detrimental habits can easily develop. Just a few of the more common ones are listed below. Some show up in physical behavior; others are purely mental. The mental ones can degrade your life just as much as the more physical ones – and they are more common.

Notice how many of the following habits are purely mental! Do you suffer from any of these - or others, not listed here?

smoking
excessive drinking
excessive coffee-drinking
drug addiction
comfort-eating
self-pity
depression
anxiety
anorexia
nail-biting
hair-pulling
fidgeting
laziness
procrastination

overspending
staying up too late at night
unwanted speech habits
excessive TV-watching
anger, including road rage
prejudice
animosity
cynicism
being overly critical
jealousy
self-deprecation
excessive gossiping
holding grudges
inconsiderate behavior

Is your life being degraded by self-defeating habits?

Detrimental habits manifest themselves as habitual actions of mind and body. All detrimental habits are essentially mental, although some result in chemical dependencies. Thankfully, even the most entrenched chemical dependencies can be overcome by changing one's thinking habits. If you can recognize a detrimental thinking habit in yourself, you have taken a key step towards a wonderful opportunity for powerful self-improvement. Some people find it hard to recognize their own self-defeating mental habits because they have conditioned themselves into believing that the habit is actually wise and beneficial. Or they have convinced themselves that the self-defeating pattern is wholly due to external factors and therefore unavoidable. The habit of self-pity is just one of the more common examples.

❖ *Self-pity is our worst enemy and if we yield to it, we can never do anything wise in this world.* —Helen Keller

Habits are affecting your fortune and potential

Our mental habits have a staggering affect on our potential and our fortune. Are you a self-made millionaire, or are you struggling to make ends meet? Whatever your answer, it is undoubtedly the result of your habits. It is your habits that make you successful or unsuccessful; likeable or unpopular; healthy or unhealthy; rich or poor; happy or unhappy!

Many unhelpful habits are formed at an early age before our intellect and sense of discernment is fully developed. And of course, the longer a habit has been in place, the harder it is to abandon. Thankfully, all habits can be changed, and they are much easier to change when you know the most effective techniques to employ.

Traditionally, people have relied on willpower to break habits. However, as most of us have discovered, willpower is anything but 'powerful'! Those who rely on it have a very low success rate when it comes to breaking deeply engrained habits such as smoking, anorexia or binge eating. I am sure you have noticed how rarely New Year's resolutions are sustained! That's because most people rely on willpower.

Willpower vs. imagination

To demonstrate how much more effective imagination is, compared to willpower, consider the following illustration.

Imagine that someone has laid a 6-inch wide, 20-foot long steel girder on some flat ground and has offered you a cash reward if you walk along the girder from one end to the other. Assuming you are not crippled or abnormally unsteady, you would do it without hesitation, wouldn't you?

Now imagine that the same girder has been laid down, bridging two skyscrapers from rooftop to rooftop. Now you are promised a briefcase full of banknotes if you walk along the girder from one skyscraper to the other. Just imagine it!

You peer over the edge, and see the traffic and bustling crowds below like so many ants, and hear the car horns echoing off the towers. It's a calm day with no wind, so the only physical difference between the two situations is the distance from the girder to the ground. The girder hasn't changed in size and you are the same person with the same abilities. So in theory, it should be just as easy to walk the length of the girder in both cases! But of course, that is not the case. Unless you are a professional steeplejack or a highly trained tightrope walker with a long balancing bar to hand, you would probably rather endure a round of Russian roulette than take up the offer! And rightly so, because you feel certain that to do so would mean certain death.

Why is this? It's purely due to what goes on in the imagination. You imagine the terror of falling off. After that, no reward on the planet will entice you to attempt the crossing. No matter how much willpower we may have, the imagination wins out every time, when it comes to governing our behavior and what we are willing to attempt. So always use imagination to your advantage, and never rely on willpower alone.

Effective techniques

For vastly improved success, we can now look to more effective means of changing our habits. Let's look at two of the most effective methods ever devised:

1) **Replacing the bad habit with actions that will become a good habit to displace the bad one.**

2) **Directly influencing the mental triggers that cause the bad habit.**

Our habitual activities are triggered deep within the subconscious regions of our mind, so the best way to change them is to go below the surface and work on those parts of our minds directly. We can do this through techniques drawn from the fields of autosuggestion and aversion therapy. Employing some willpower is helpful too, but to rely on willpower alone will probably result in failure.

For our illustrative bad habit, let's take smoking since it is considered one of the toughest to break. I personally used these techniques in combination to quit smoking over thirty years ago and have not resumed since. These techniques work equally well for any habit you seek to change. Let's look at the first technique...

1) Displace a poor habit with new, beneficial one!

❖ *A nail is driven out by another nail.*

Habit is overcome by habit. —Desiderius Erasmus

I used the word 'displace' because it describes what takes place using this method. The reason this method works so well is that due to our nature, we can only perform one conscious thought or action at a time. All you need to do to implement this technique is to remember to nip the unwanted behavior in the bud by replacing it with wanted, beneficial, useful behavior.

You alone can decide which unwanted habit you wish to focus on removing first. When you have decided, then next thing to do is to decide on the beneficial, action, behavior or activity you will use to replace the unwanted behavior.

To do this effectively, I suggest you refer back to the personal goals and long-term ambitions you listed in your A-Log. Refer also to your 'to do' list, for things you can do to advance yourself towards those goals and ambitions.

Now, as soon as you notice yourself beginning to display the unwanted behavior, immediately (before the unwanted behavior is completed or fully embarked upon), engage in the desirable activity instead. In order to get into the habit of doing this without fail, you may need to do some self-programming of your subconscious mind, and that will be covered in the next technique.

Apart from its efficacy, another great thing about this technique is that you can use it to kill two birds with one stone. Let me give you an example. When I gave up smoking, thirty years ago, every time I sensed myself reaching for a cigarette, I immediately engaged in some tidying up of my workspace. By keeping this up for two or three weeks, I not only quit smoking, but gained the good habit of tidying up!

We can use the same techniques to ditch all types of habit. All it takes is a little self-control aided by suitable techniques. If self-control is difficult, then work on it bit by bit. Like a muscle, it will get stronger as you exercise it.

2) Change the unwanted behavior at source

As already mentioned, habitual behavior is triggered within the subconscious part of our mind. People usually don't reach for a cigarette, bite their nails or curse the wife after making a conscious tactical decision to do so; they initiate the action subconsciously, by force of habit. They have programmed their subconscious mind to behave in that way. So the way to change these subconscious triggers is to reprogram the part of the subconscious mind where they occur. Another chapter in this book explores ways of doing this in greater depth, but here I will summarize one of the most effective methods for changing bad habits. It works on the relevant part of the subconscious mind, borrowing techniques from the psychiatric field of aversion therapy.

As we have mentioned elsewhere in this book, the subconscious mind pays attention to things which are: <u>repeated frequently</u> and <u>accompanied by strong emotion.</u>

These two qualities are what the subconscious mind looks for to distinguish input to be acted-upon, as opposed to input it will rate as unimportant.

Preparing for effective self-reprogramming

We can use the following method to effectively change unwanted habits by reprogramming our subconscious mind. The twofold secret of success is firstly to plan our session in advance, and secondly, to carry out the actual session in optimal conditions so that our programming takes root in the subconscious mind. We will plan our strategy in advance so that we know what to do when we are deeply relaxed in a distraction-free environment. (By so doing, we won't need to disrupt our deeply relaxed state in order to ponder over the best methodology to employ.)

Prepare your programming tactic in advance

1) Decide on the aversion specifics to employ

In preparation for some effective reprogramming, think of some disturbing, unhappy imagery connected with the potential consequences of the bad habit we wish to remove. The more heart-wrenchingly fearful and unpleasant the imagery, the better. Case in point: remember our illustration of the girder-walking challenge? It was merely the imagination of the intense shock and fear of falling that halted the inclination to take up the challenge. See how well it works! It was the emotion (in this case, fear) that did it.

Then we want to connect the fearful, obnoxious, or repulsive imagery with the bad habit in question. In the case of the smoker, I recommend first imagining the very beginnings of the impulse to reach for a cigarette, perhaps accompanied by the smell of cigarette smoke – and then immediately vividly imagine the situation of having to face lung surgery with a 50/50 chance of survival. For best results, it needs to be something that actually stirs your emotions to the extent of causing some noticeable physical reaction. Perhaps you could imagine waking up during the surgery and seeing your own opened chest and the tarry, horrendous state of your own lungs... Or imagine one of your closest loved ones being operated-on because they caught cancer from your own tobacco smoke... Obviously, you will modify this technique to suit the habit you wish to drop.

2) Decide on the replacement behavior to adopt

Also in advance of your reprogramming session, consider what beneficial behavior you want to adopt, to replace the unwanted behavior.

3) Envisage the ultimate benefits of succeeding

Now think of some absolutely wonderful, heart-warming, sublime benefits you can mentally attach to this alternative behavior. The stronger and more positive the emotion this invokes, the better.

4) Minimize distractions

In order to get the subconscious mind to adopt our new programming during our forthcoming autosuggestion session, it helps greatly to create suitable conditions for effective communication with that part of the mind. That means reducing distractions to a minimum. The subconscious mind is much more likely to listen to our new programming when we have its undivided attention. Otherwise it will be like trying to converse with a bus driver while he is circumnavigating Piccadilly Circus at rush hour!

Distractions can be external or internal. External distractions include phones ringing, noisy neighbors, TV, music and most other sensory input coming from outside our bodies. Then there are internal distractions, including the clamor and commotion of our chattering intellect, some of which is conscious and some of which is subconscious. So pay careful attention to catch the subconscious activity.

Deep relaxation is the means we can employ for subduing the inner commotion until stillness of mind is reached. Full relaxation and thinking cannot coexist, because thoughts cause tensions in our bodies. Become aware of this. By deliberately relaxing deeply, we automatically subdue our conscious and subconscious mental activity.

5) Implement your session!

As soon as the opportunity arises, get down to your first autosuggestion session. Lie flat on the floor with something comfortable underneath you, such as a duvet and pillow, and perhaps a blanket over you for warmth. I recommend lying on a covered floor rather than a bed, since a bed can trigger the mental patterns we fall into when we go to bed at night. We don't typically lie on the floor, so it tends not to trigger drowsiness the way lying on a bed can.

Once positioned as comfortably as possible, start to progressively relax your mind and body so that your intellectual activity is subdued as much as possible. Then, when you are as relaxed as you can become, through focused intent, bring to mind those vivid images you prepared earlier. Through visualization, connect those feelings of revulsion, fear and dread with the habit you wish to drop. Then, imagine yourself replacing the unwanted habitual behavior with the beneficial alternative behavior (mental or physical) that you have decided upon in the previous stage, and imagine enjoying the wonderful benefits of the new behavior.

By this method you can progressively reprogram your subconscious mind so that when you start having the impulse to engage the bad habit, the alarming imagery will be subconsciously triggered and will intercept the behavior before it takes hold. And you will also automatically remember to enact the new behavior to replace the unwanted behavior. Repeated often enough, this soon becomes a new and beneficial pattern that happens automatically.

For this to work most effectively, I recommend that you repeat the deep relaxation with auto-suggestion sessions more than once every day until your habits are under control. An excellent time to practice would be first thing in the morning as soon as you are wide awake, and last thing at night, before you become drowsy. If you add one session around the middle of the day too, you will be doubly successful.

Make no mistake, this procedure is pure dynamite and you can use it to change your life in all sorts of desirable ways. Persistence is the key. Keep improving your technique and become familiar with how it works. Notice how imagination has so much more influence over subconscious behavior than willpower alone.

Be vigilant

Once you start to enjoy success with the approaches covered here, it's important to sustain the practice. It's helpful to remember that certain situations render us vulnerable to falling back into unwanted habits. Driving when you are in a hurry to get somewhere quickly can trigger some people's vulnerability to road rage tendencies. Those who once habitually lit up a cigarette whenever they imbibed at the local pub may find themselves very vulnerable when in that environment. Learn to recognize these trigger situations and try to avoid them. If you can't avoid them, then double your guard when you encounter them.

You can also use situational cues as reminders to perform actions that you want to become habit. To establish a new habit, it can be very helpful to tie it to an event that happens regularly as a matter of course. Perhaps you could decide to do your daily reading or tidying-up immediately after the 9-o'clock news, or write up your diary each day after your evening meal or listen to educative audio books while driving to work.

Persist in the face of temporary failure!

People sometimes lose heart and give up as soon as they experience their first relapse into an old habit. Don't make this mistake. And beware of the tendency to find excuses for giving up. A temporary failure or two is not a good reason to give up! Just ease yourself back onto the rails and continue on your chosen trajectory! You should feel encouraged, because you have already started developing the skills needed to defeat the habit. I think I finally gave up smoking permanently on my third attempt. The first attempt was by far the hardest and most short-lived. Each subsequent attempt became easier because I had already developed the mental skills needed to ditch the habit.

RECOMMENDED ACTION STEPS

1) Observe yourself very carefully throughout each day in order to identify any unhelpful mental habits as well as the more physical ones. This self-awareness is, in itself a new habit to adopt! If you forget to implement it, why not use the techniques we have covered, to make it stick!

2) In your A-Log, develop and regularly review a list of the habits you want to drop.

3) Using the techniques described in this chapter, start unloading your unwanted habits and replace them with helpful, useful, rewarding ones!

8
SAUCEDARTS
NEUTRALIZE YOUR WORRIES

❖ *You can't wring your hands and roll up your sleeves at the same time.* —Pat Schroeder

This chapter introduces another great tool. This one will help you whenever the quality of your life is marred by some worry or other. Perhaps that worry is blatantly clear, or perhaps it is simmering away at a subconscious level but still getting you down and sapping your zest for living. Perhaps you have grown to accept it, or have even become addicted to it – or perhaps you have just given up trying to find the solution. The S.A.U.C.E.D.A.R.T.S device is powerful tool for dealing with worries.

Imagine this: You were on a flight to Peru and your plane developed a mechanical fault while crossing the Yutacan Peninsula. It was forced to crash-land somewhere amid the jungles of Guatemala. You are one of the only survivors. You are now very worried. The plane's radio is a smoldering wreck and you could be hundreds of miles from civilization! But now you have a much more immediate worry: You have just seen a large black jaguar (the furry kind) slinking down a nearby hillside, heading in your direction! It has probably picked up your scent and has you earmarked as its next meal! You look around for ideas and you notice one other survivor of the crash nearby. You call out to him and point out the big cat coming in your direction.

"Hey, no problemo" says the tanned, Latino. He reaches into his rucksack and pulls out a blowpipe! From a side pocket he produces a dart. He then fishes out a small jar filled with what looks like a brown sauce. He unscrews the top and dips one of the darts into the sauce and loads it into the blowpipe. The subject of your fear is now poised at the other side of the large clearing and now it's running towards you with gathering speed, with its eyes locked onto yours, transfixing you to the spot where you stand. He is primed for the kill. Just in time, your native companion levels his blowpipe, and *PPHHOOOTT!* The sauce-dipped dart sails through the air and finds its mark in the jaguar's shoulder! The cat starts losing momentum as it crosses the clearing, and when he is only a few yards from you, it collapses into a flaccid heap, thoroughly neutralized! Such is the power of S.A.U.C.E.D.A.R.T.S!

Worry is neither effective nor enjoyable, and sustained pressures can stress you out and reduce your effectiveness and certainly undermine the pleasure of living. A period of anxiety can be a miserable time for anyone. Most importantly perhaps, prolonged anxiety and excessive pressure can be detrimental to your health.

Psychologist Dr. Dorothy McCoy, summarizes the dangers in her article, *The Evolution of Worry*:

Every system in your body is affected by worry. In addition to raising blood pressure and increasing blood clotting, worry can prompt your liver to produce more cholesterol, all of which can raise your risk of heart attack and stroke. Muscle tension can give rise to headaches, back pain, and other body aches. Worry can also trigger an increase in stomach acid and either slow or speed up muscle contractions in your intestines, which can lead to stomach aches, constipation, diarrhea, gas or heartburn. Worry can affect your skin (rash or itch). It can impact your respiratory system by aggravating asthma. Growing evidence even suggests that chronic worry can compromize your immune system, making you more vulnerable to bacteria, viruses, perhaps even cancer.

Worry, fear and pressure also reduce clear thinking; a worried mind can go round and round in circles covering the same ground, getting nowhere. When overwhelmed with worries, one can become unsure about how to deal with it all in the quickest and most effective way. That's why I devised this magical rescue key to tackle these situations. It's a reliable and universal key you can always turn to when the going gets heavy or when you start feeling overwhelmed.

S.A.U.C.E.D.A.R.T.S.

Here are the steps to take:

1) Specify: Identify or define exactly what is worrying/pressuring you. Keep a notebook with you for this purpose so you can write down everything you find yourself worrying about. This will help you identify your worries.

2) Adapt: Learn to accept what you cannot change. Decide which causes of anxiety are beyond your control. Face up to them and look for ways to make these pressures more tolerable. It has been said that maturity is the art of living in peace with that which we cannot change.

3) Urgency: Look at the issues that you do have some control over and list them in order of importance and urgency. To help evaluate the urgency, you may wish to consider what is the worst that could happen if each of the issues remains unresolved.

4) Courses of action: Write down a list of possible courses of action you could take that would eliminate, or at least reduce, these anxieties.

5) Easiest: List your worries and their possible solutions, in order of the ease with which you could eliminate or tackle them.

6) Decide which course(s) of action you will take, and in what order, to tackle the worrying or pressing issues.

7) Act upon your chosen course of remedy. You can implement one action at a time, or you can tackle more than one concurrently if you wish.

Do what seems most appropriate. Be decisive; once you have decided on your course of action, follow through decisively and don't hesitate. Action fosters courage.

8) **Review** your progress. Is your action plan working effectively? If not, decide how best to tweak it and try again.

9) **Tweak** your action plan to make it more effective.

10) **Succeed** with your refined action plan.

Compact version for your wallet

To help you remember the process, copy the following simplified version onto a piece of card to keep in your wallet:

S.A.U.C.E.D.A.R.T.S.

Specify or define exactly what is pressuring you.
Adapt: Learn to live with what you can't change.
Urgency: List your worries in order of importance.
Courses of action: List the possible courses of action.
Easiest: Rank the worries according to ease of remedy.
Decide which course(s) of action you will take.
Act: Implement your chosen course(s) of action.
Review the situation regularly. Is your plan working?
Tweak: If your plan isn't working effectively, tweak it.
Succeed with your new or improved action plan.

Let the new dawn fire you up!

Now when you wake up in the morning, relish the new day, thankful that you have a plan for tackling the issues at hand. Today is the first day of the rest of your life, so make it a step forward in an improving life-situation. Get busy with your chosen action plan at every opportunity. Occupation and full involvement are often the best antidote for worry and other negative emotions—and knowing you are doing what you can to deal with things that worry you, fosters hope, courage and optimism; and that makes you more effective. It's a win-win situation. Avoid the worry rut!

Prolonged anxiety is bad for your health, so don't make a habit of it! Using the above ten-step procedure is a healthy habit to adopt. From now on, spend your energies on remedial action rather than fruitless worry.

Anxiety disorders

If you find it impossible to determine what it is that's worrying you, it could be that you have an anxiety disorder that would benefit from medical attention. One variety of anxiety disorder is what the medical profession calls generalized anxiety disorder (GAD). This usually occurs when too many things have caused you anxiety over a prolonged period, and you have gradually become settled into an engrained pattern of anxiety that persists even when there is nothing specific to worry about. If you think you have developed this fairly common disorder, you can work at changing the habits of thought and emotion that manifest the symptoms. Read carefully the chapters in this book covering thinking and the mind.

For most people however, worry is usually caused by something specific that can easily be identified. In this case, you can deploy SAUCEDARTS!

Gather all the information you need

When you become aware of being worried, do your best to identify and define the course of your anxiety. Make sure you have all the information you need to decide on possible workable and effective solutions. If you are lacking any relevant information, make every effort to get it, so that you are properly equipped to devise effective remedial actions.

Mentally step outside of the situation

If you are intensely worried, your emotional involvement may interfere with your ability to think optimally about the issue. One way of reducing this problem is to imagine you are gathering the information on behalf of someone else. For example, imagine you are a private detective acting on behalf of a client.

Sometimes the course of action you settle upon will be complex, involving more than one simple step. In this case, break down the course of action into logical steps and implement them one by one. By doing so, the task becomes much easier and less daunting.

❖ *In the midst of chaos, there is also opportunity. —Sun Tzu*

One day at a time

If a course of action is going to take some time to complete, set out to tackle it one day at a time. Dale Carnegie advised: *"Live in day-tight compartments. No matter how bad your current situation, you only have to put up with it until bedtime. Tomorrow is a new day and you will tackle that when it arrives."*

Your aim should be such that when you go to bed, you can rest at peace, knowing you have done the best you could do in the circumstances. Before you go to sleep, write down the six most important things you intend to accomplish or tackle the following day with regard to dealing with your anxieties and eliminating their causes. Then let go of it all and sleep well!

Breaking the pattern of worry

If ever you find yourself brooding and becoming negative or pessimistic, do whatever you can to break the pattern. Psychologists call this a pattern-interrupt. It is a valuable tactic because if you get stuck in a rut of worry, your problem-solving skills may decline.

I was down on my luck once as a youngster. I was in a foreign country with only a few coins left to my name after losing my wallet. My future looked bleak. I was anxious and worried. Night was closing in. How could I use those few coins to improve my predicament? I couldn't think of anything practical I could do, apart from saving the coins to purchase food when I next became hungry. Acting on a whim, however, I cast care to the wind and used up the coins on an absorbing video game in an amusement arcade. Doing so switched my mind into an alert and effective but amused problem-solving mode (it was a tank-battle game by Atari, back in the days when video games were in their infancy). Within half an hour of leaving that amusement arcade, I walked into a hotel, prompted by a hunch, and asked if they needed any staff. I was offered a job on the spot. Problem solved! When you are worrying, your mind is typically going round and round in circles like a chicken with its head cut off. So do what you can to snap yourself out of the worrying mode.

Don't worry about the past!

A word about the past and the future: Learn not to worry about past events. The past cannot be changed, so regard past events as a learning experience. Let go of past regrets and move on, a wiser person. Regarding future events, always remember the old adage: "It may never happen." As the wise man said: "Don't let yesterday and tomorrow rob you of today."

RECOMMENDED ACTION STEP

Practice applying the SAUCEDARTS technique to your life situation. If you don't have any worries or pressures degrading the quality of your life, practice it anyway so that you will be better equipped to use it whenever worries and pressures do encumber or overwhelm you in the future.

PART TWO

CONDITIONING YOUR MIND FOR BETTER OUTCOMES

Now that your flight plan is clear and you have decided on your desired destinations, we can take an exciting step forward into Part Two. Part Two is all about improving you, the one and only! This part teaches you special transformational techniques in addition to the basics - including how the master controls work and how the autopilot system works.

With this part under your belt, you will be able to stay 'airborne' comfortably for extended periods. You will learn to attend to the most important things so you don't fall foul of storms and turbulence. It will help you negotiate mountain ranges and war zones, staying in control of your destiny. It confers the psychological skills you'll need as an outstanding high flyer.

❖ *Our life is what our thoughts make it. —Marcus Aurelius*

9
THINKING ABOUT THINKING
OPTIMIZE YOUR MINDSCAPE

❖ *The aim of education should be to teach us how to think, rather than what to think.* —James Beattie

The primary factor that enables us to enjoy successful, happy lives is the way we think, i.e. our habitual thinking patterns and the language we use for our thinking and speaking. This part of the course is about optimizing your mind and your thinking for success and self-fulfillment. In this chapter, we take a general overview of optimizing our mindscape for optimal success and self-fulfillment. This chapter prepares us for those that follow.

Much of our thinking is governed by force of habit. Many of these habits are adopted at an early age, copied from family members and early role models. Some of these habitual ways of thinking and feeling may not be in our best interests. Many people are stuck in self-defeating thought patterns and emotional habits. Many lean towards pessimism and have a low opinion of themselves. They feel like victims of life. The voice of their adopted inner critic is constantly undermining their self-belief. An inner critic is not a bad thing, but we don't want it to distort the truth or run amok. An inner critic is only an inner critic. It's there to serve, not to rule the roost.

Negative, self-defeating styles of thinking and feeling have been around since man first crawled out of the green slime of Jurassic Park and complained that no-one had provided any soap to wash the green slime off with! Such thinking styles are thus well established and still considered the norm in many circles. They are often so deeply ingrained and habitual that most people aren't aware of them until someone points them out or questions their validity. They do most of their dirty-work below the level of conscious awareness.

Progress begins with unlearning

Mental and emotional habits, no matter how deeply ingrained, can be broken. By consciously and deliberately adopting healthy, constructive habits of thought and emotion, we can truly transform our lives and experience amazing changes in our fortunes. We then cease being victims, and take charge of our thinking and of our lives and become truly happy.

Inner talk can consist of feelings as well as words

Much of our inner self-talk that goes on below the level of conscious awareness isn't actually articulated into words, but takes the form of feelings. Remember that feelings and words are both forms of language. Feelings and emotions are the universal language that all living creatures understand and inter-communicate with. That's why humans often form such a close bond with a pet. And it's why you can still have empathic communication even in a country where you don't know a single word of the national language.

Awareness of self-talk is key

By becoming aware of your self-talk you can change it. You can experience wonderful changes in your fortunes if you make a point of becoming aware of the nature and tone of your self-talk—and indeed your interpersonal talk, and take steps to improve it.

Realize that the first conclusions you tend to jump to are not always the only ones—or the best ones. And events you might immediately look upon as bad luck can often be valuable opportunities if you look deeper.

Be proactive rather than reactive

Some are irrefutably infortunate. However, if you cannot find a cloud's silver lining, you can still choose how you react to it. You could wallow in self-pity or self-blame and brood upon the situation, but that doesn't help. The other choice is to focus immediately on what you can do to improve your situation, and take action accordingly. In other words, be proactive rather than just reactive. When you transform any tendency you have to react negatively into a tendency to react constructively, everything changes for the better. By reacting negatively, I mean indulging in any unhelpful, unpleasant emotions that have no practical benefit. Taking positive action to improve the situation immediately gives rise to self-respect, encouragement and other helpful emotions. Of course, with some kinds of misfortune, your power to improve the situation may be very limited, but by exercising what power you do have, your sphere of influence can be progressively increased.

Positive action invokes a positive attitude

Most people wait until they are thinking positively before taking some positive action. If you adopt this approach, you may be waiting around for a long time without getting anywhere. A key observation of success is that by engaging in positive action, you naturally invoke positive thoughts and ideas. Positive action lifts your attitude. Remember that! The best way to purge a negative attitude is to get stuck into some wisely-selected, positive action or program of actions.

Frame everything in positive language

So what is an easy way to think positively about everything? There is one method that works really well: Get into the habit of framing everything in positive language! Adopting this one simple habit will bring phenomenal changes in your fortune if you have not already done so! Another important habit that improves people's lives like magic is learning to habitually look for the positive in everything, and the value in every experience.

Changing longstanding mental habits is a challenge; it takes sustained determination - especially when the people around you are self-assured in traditional negative ways. You'll need to train yourself not to follow 'the herd' when 'the herd' subscribes to *Chisolm's Law* which says: *"Any time that things appear to be getting better, you have overlooked something!"* Equally negative and self-defeating, is *Murphy's Law* which says: *"Nothing is as easy as it looks; everything takes longer than you expect; and if anything can go wrong, it will, and at the worst possible moment."* You may find those amusing, but such are the beliefs of the negative thinker and the loser! If you entertain such notions, they will become your reality because the unconscious part of your mind, which governs your hormones and emotional demeanor, takes on board anything you repeatedly tell it. That's why repeating positive affirmations is a fantastic idea. By repeating something, it eventually affects one's subconscious belief system, with far-reaching consequences.

So get the habit of spending more time considering the possible good outcomes of any situation, and less time imagining bad outcomes. Consider how you might succeed—not just how you might fail. Think of the things you'd like to achieve and consider how you might succeed rather than how you might fail. Reflect on your past successes rather than lamenting your past failures. Cultivate good feelings, instead of wallowing in negative ones. If someone behaves negatively towards you, consider that it could be due to an unhappy event in their life and not something you should take personally.

Every coin has two sides, and every time you look for the positive side, you are strengthening your success potential and your personal power. By looking at the positive and beneficial side of things, you neutralize those negative emotions that would otherwise have defeated you. This is so important, because negative emotions slow us down, lower our energy and our available IQ, and limit our effectiveness. Good emotions give us energy, mental alacrity, intelligence and inspiration. Negative thinking can also result from fatigue, so if you start thinking negatively because you're tired, get some rest if you possibly can. Practice deep relaxation to recoup your energies rapidly and free your mind of residual negativity.

ERASE negative self-defeating self-talk that you notice

This technique is invaluable in the process of nullifying negative self-talk that you notice. As soon as you notice your inner talk saying something that is detrimental to your positivity or self-esteem, such as "I can't do that", when in fact there is no real reason why you can't do it and when it would benefit you to do it; or "I can't face that crowd tonight", when you know from experience that evenings with that crowd often turn out to be worthwhile and enjoyable, here is what to do: Immediately say to yourself (aloud if practical) "ERASE" – just as if you are sending a command to erase some faulty computer programming. It also helps if you visualize yourself pushing a big button printed with the word "ERASE". This will often completely nullify the faulty programming. Then immediately follow that with a positive affirmation to the opposite effect of the unwanted, bad programming statement.

Nourish your mind with positive input

Nourishing your mind with other people's positive thoughts and ideas is like feeding your body with healthy nourishing food. It makes you healthy. Turn away from all pessimistic, cynical input. Don't allow yourself to be a receptacle for other people's complaints and negative thinking; you won't be doing yourself, or them, a favor. Refuse to get caught up in pointless arguments, antagonism, bitterness, regret, anger, jealousy, sorrow, annoyance, depression, or any other negative emotions. Read positive books. Be vigilant about how you are allowing yourself to be programmed! Television has a powerful hypnotic influence over our attitudes, so if you choose to spend your valuable time watching television, at least take care to watch only positive programs that actually help you to achieve your most important objectives. Talk to positive-minded successful people. If you are in a social rut, and surrounded by mediocre people with mediocre minds, don't let them drag you down. Instead, make a massive effort to spend time among interesting, inspiring people - people you can admire, learn from and be inspired by - people who support your goals and ambitions. Hunt them down. Make friends with them. Work with them. Break out of the old social habits. Join a different club, group or society; get a different job; do whatever it takes.

Positive thoughts and emotions, besides affecting one's fortunes, have positive health benefits, whereas persistent negativity tends to be bad for one's physical, not to mention mental, health.

Ancient masters of the mind taught this too!

❖ *When disturbed by negative thoughts, opposite [positive] ones should be thought of.* —*Yoga Sutras of Patanjali, 2.33*

The above technique is more or less what is known as 'cognitive behavioral therapy' by today's psychiatric profession and is considered by many to be the panacea for most mental and emotional problems. The yogis of India have also been using another 'modern' technique for thousands of years: the affirmation, which in the yogic tradition is called a mantra. To overcome states of mental turmoil, they repeat mantras such as 'shanti' (meaning 'peace'). We can use affirmations to our advantage. When you catch yourself thinking a negative, self-defeating, destructive thought, you can immediately displace it by affirming the opposite (just as Patanjali prescribed). Repeating the positive, opposite thought over and over displaces the negative thought, and overwrites the unwanted programming with the new. You cannot focus on two things at once, so the most effective way to ditch an unwanted thought or habit is to replace it with another thought or habit. Paradise can be here and now!

Whether we are in heaven or hell is down to where we focus our attention and how we think and communicate our thoughts. The greatest mental masters of history have pointed this out. Jesus Christ purportedly said: "The kingdom of God is within you." (Luke 17:21)

❖ *His disciples asked him, "When will the kingdom come?" Jesus said, "It will not come by waiting for it. It will not be a matter of saying 'Here it is' or 'There it is'. Rather, the kingdom of the father is spread out upon the earth, and people do not see it."* —Gos. Thom. 113

This book is not intended to be a religious guide, but it is worth noting some of the gems of higher insight found in some of the world's scriptures.

There are two ways of looking at any situation you are in: You can regard your cup as half full or half empty! Actually there are more than two ways: You can also choose to realize that your cup runneth over!

Learning to be thankful for all the fortunate things in your situation and life is the attitude of the wise person. One of the most effective and proven ways to develop an attitude of gratitude is to spend a few minutes, every day, writing down six things you are grateful for. This habit will have fantastic effects on your outlook and your circumstances if you haven't already adopted it. It's a good idea to get into the habit of doing it at the same time and place every day. Bedtime is a particularly suitable time for some.

Change your life by changing your language!

One of the best ways to learn new and positive thinking patterns that will transform your life is to get into the habit of framing everything in positive language. This single habit can affect your fortunes and your inner wellbeing in fabulous ways! A friend of mine made the decision to eliminate the word 'no' from her vocabulary, and from that point, she never looked back. She then took it a step further and started to replace low-energy words with high-energy words, and this further affected her fortunes and her outcomes. I tried it for myself and have never looked back! Every negative word we think and speak, adversely affects our emotional state, vitality and inner power. Positive words do the opposite. So start using all the high-energy, positive words you can and weed out the low-energy and negative ones!

Use uplifting words!
Fabulous, fantastic, brilliant, adorable, wonderful, phenomenal, superb, terrific, supreme, miraculous, marvelous, terrific, spectacular, incredible, sublime, ecstatic, love, loving, loveable, sweet, beautiful, righteous, amazing, divine, awesome, heavenly...

Why use a mediocre word when an uplifting word can be used to good effect? Switch negative statements into more positive ones. Think and speak of challenges rather than problems. Every word that the conscious mind utters has actual electrochemical and hormonal affects in the body. So immerse yourself in all the good uplifting words and thoughts you can, every minute of every day, and you will be amazed by the results.

You can use phrases like 'not good' in place of 'bad'. The unconscious mind tends to notice the main adjective or noun while disregarding the 'not' because 'not' isn't the kind of word that involves an image or a feeling. By using the single word 'bad', you feed the subconscious mind with a pure negative which would to some extent trigger the fight or flight response (even if only slightly), thus blocking access to your higher mind.

Listen only to positive music
Like television programming, music has a powerful hypnotic affect on our outlook, our thinking and our

attitudes. Therefore it is wise to listen only to positive music with positive lyrics and/or positive melodies that evoke positive feelings, ideas and images.

- *Great men are those who see that thoughts rule the world.*
  —Ralph Waldo Emerson

- *Look at things, not as they are, but as they can be. Visualization adds value to everything. A big thinker always visualizes what can be done in the future.*
  —David J. Schwartz, Ph.D.

RECOMMENDED ACTION STEPS

1) Become aware of your self-talk. Remember, self-talk is often just a feeling that you haven't quite verbalized. Question your self-talk constantly. Don't let it have the final say if it seems negative or counter-productive. Replace negative self-talk with consciously-directed positive self talk. Eliminate negative words from your self-talk! Use as many uplifting words as you can.

2) Pin some slips of paper up around your home or office saying: "I FRAME EVERYTHING IN POSITIVE TERMS."

3) In your A-Log record every kind of self-talk that you become aware of. Write down all the ways you can improve that internal dialogue.

4) In your A-Log, list any positive actions you can take that are likely to change your attitude for the better.

5) Every day, write down six things you are grateful for.

6) Consider carefully the kind of programming you are absorbing through television, literature and the music you listen to. From now on, be very selective, and look forward to big improvements in your wellbeing and effectiveness.

7) Weed out any songs from your music collection that have negative, sad, morbid, self-pitying or negative lyrics, however seductive they may be.

10
BYPASS THE BOUNCER!
& OTHER SELF-PROGRAMMING TIPS

❖ *Like the wind that carries one ship east and another west, the law of autosuggestion will lift you up or pull you down according to the way that you set your sails of thought.*
—Napoleon Hill

Every minute of every day, someone out there wants to program us to their own ends. How much better we can do in life if we reprogram ourselves to our own ends! This chapter looks at the way all of us have been programmed and it looks at powerful techniques for self-programming that you can adopt for tremendous benefits according to your wishes.

We've all heard of it but not everyone understands it. The subconscious part of our mind has tremendous influence over how we behave and the 'luck' we attract. It's the part of our mind that enables us to carry out complicated tasks automatically without conscious thinking. It governs our moods and our attitudes without us having any awareness of its constant activity.

It is like a central computer that performs according to how it has been programmed. It even runs our biological processes and forms part of the sympathetic nervous system controlling our hormones and regulating our heartbeat, breathing and other automatic bodily functions. Its primary purpose is to keep us alive and in good health.

Early programming

As mentioned elsewhere, much of our early behavioral programming took place long ago when we were very young and impressionable. Prior to the age of about eleven, our intellect and its powers of rational discernment were not fully developed. Prior to around that age, we tended to accept whatever we were told by our trusted guardians or other authority figures. If a teacher told us we were 'hopeless' at arithmetic while in junior school, we regarded such judgments as the unavoidable truth. So after that, it seemed pointless to make an effort. It became our internal programming which undermined our math aptitudes.

The faulty programming affecting our lives is not available in print anywhere for us to refer to; we have to rely on clues and deductions as evidence that it exists. When it is evident that we have been wrongly programmed (that is to say, we exhibit behaviors that we don't want), we can actually overwrite the old self-defeating programming with new programs that result in the behavior we want. This is fantastic news, and a cause for great hope.

❖ *Learn to unlearn! —Benjamin Disraeli*

Yes, we can definitely reprogram ourselves! However, there is an art and science to doing it effectively. Affirmations are one tool for accomplishing this. However, to use them effectively, one needs to understand a few things about how the mind works.

Meet the bouncer!

The chief saboteur of the affirmation is what we might call our inner critic. The inner critic decides what our subconscious mind will accept as truth and what it should reject as unimportant or untrue. It sorts the wheat from the chaff... or at least, that is what it is supposed to do. (It is not infallible.) This is the subconscious mind's gatekeeper. It is like the bouncer at a high class nightclub door, whose job is to allow only important people into the club and refuse entry to fakes, charlatans and riff-raff.

If you repeat over and over: "I am a millionaire" in the hope that the subconscious mind will help bring about that situation, what tends to happen is that this inner critic or gatekeeper does exactly what he is employed to do: he intervenes and affirms something to the effect of: "Pull the other one; it plays Jingle Bells!"

The subconscious mind is like the club owner; he trusts the bouncer to do his job. He trusts the bouncer's discretion and otherwise pays little attention to the affirmation seeking to gain entry. There are a number of ways we can bypass the bouncer to get our chosen affirmation through the club's door and to be accepted as an important and valid participant in the event going on inside.

Avoid blatant untruths

Many people have poor success with affirmations because they don't understand how the mind works. Instead of trying to implant the suggestion "I am a millionaire", you might affirm: *"I choose to act in ways that bring me ever-increasing wealth."* This is much more effective, because it is impossible for the bouncer to refute such a statement. That's because it's not blatantly untrue, provided there is an honest intention behind the affirmation.

Try affirming a single word

Joseph Murphy, in his pivotal book *The Power of the Subconscious Mind*, recommends simply repeating the word 'WEALTH' at every opportunity, because the subconscious part of the mind cannot refute a word (such as 'wealth') in isolation. The yogis of India repeat mantras which often consist of a single word to this effect. For example: 'shanti' (meaning peace). Buddhists often repeat a single phrase such as 'loving kindness' as a form of self-suggestion in this way. You can pick an abstract noun of your choosing – whatever quality you wish to dominate your mindset, and start to influence your inner nature.

Employ emotion and repetition

The gatekeeper of the subconscious mind looks for two key signals to determine whether cognitive input is to be admitted as true and important. The two main factors it looks for when exercising such discernment are (a) ***repetition*** (if some declaration is repeated, it's more likely to be true and important); and (b) ***strong emotion*** (if an incoming statement has strong emotion attached to it, it is much more likely to be important).

The importance of emotion

The unconscious mind pays attention to what we imagine, as well as what we actually perceive - especially when strong emotion is part of the package.

We've all heard the saying, 'A picture paints a thousand words.' This applies also to subconscious programming. If your affirmation consists of imagery rather than words, it will be more effective. Imagery is harder for our swarthy bouncer to refute. Worded affirmations only work insofar as they evoke emotion.

The words that can carry the strongest emotions are nouns, verbs and adjectives. As you probably know, nouns are the words that name 'things', e.g. cat, car, house, knife, pen, happiness, sadness, health, sickness, etc. Adjectives give further descriptive information about a noun, e.g. big, small, happy, sad, lovely, nasty, healthy, unhealthy, etc. The more emotion a word evokes, in your mind, the more your inner gatekeeper will consider it worthy of filing away, rubber-stamped as 'important'.

Using repetition

The other signal that the gatekeeper looks out for when deciding whether input may be important enough to pay attention to, is *repetition*. If it receives some input from the conscious part of the mind, unless that message is highly charged with powerful emotion, it will tend to ignore it. However, if that message is repeated often enough, it starts to pay attention and considers: "Could this be something that needs acting upon?" However, it should be stressed that repetition alone is often not enough. Repeating an affirmation just once with total belief and strong emotion is far more powerful than repeating it one a hundred times, knowing that it's untrue. This is another reason why many people get the impression that affirmations don't work. They give the idea a try, but give up too soon, and probably don't employ emotion or employ suitable techniques to fool the bouncer.

Methods of delivery

There are several ways to deliver affirmations. You can repeat a statement to yourself verbally, or better still, by mental imagery, as already mentioned. You can also make a recording and listen to it while relaxing, or when drifting off to sleep. You might want to consider leaving the recording switched to 'repeat' so that it plays over and over from the moment you get into bed to the moment you get dressed in the morning. Then it will be playing during that period when your mind is in the so-called 'alpha-wave state', when you are drifting off to sleep and when you are transitioning back to wakefulness in the morning.

You can also write carefully-worded affirmations on pieces of paper and pin them up in places where you can't fail to see them as you go about your daily routines. There are even computer programs that will display your chosen affirmations on your computer screen repeatedly for a fraction of a second at a time. Such subliminal programming can be very effective. Although little emotion is involved, it seems that it's possible to 'bypass the bouncer' by sneaking through the door when he's not looking!

Use the stairs!

I have found a wonderful use for stairs; I repeat positive affirmations while I ascend them. I repeat an affirmation every time a foot projects me upwards. For the duration of my ascent, I repeat, "**happier, happier, happier**" or "**healthier, healthier, healthier**" and feel it with strong positive emotion. There is a significant symbolism to ascending stairs which helps to impress and convince the subconscious mind's gatekeeper.

Neutralize the bouncer!

If you can somehow distract the bouncer or put him to sleep, he will no longer be able to perform his duties. The more you can subdue this inner critic, the less there will be to obstruct your desired programming. How can we accomplish this? One way is to carry out the desired reprogramming while we are deeply relaxed. Intellectual activity and deep relaxation don't coexist. This is why hypnotherapists induce deep relaxation before starting to deliver their programming. A still mind has no intellectual activity taking place. The bouncer takes a break!

The sensory gating system

Psychologists talk about the sensory gating system (SGS for short). Our senses are bombarded with about 40 million bits of information! However, our brains are only capable of registering about one millionth of that amount. It is the job of the SGS to pick out what it regards as the important and relevant bits of information coming in via the senses. It makes its choices based on how the subconscious mind has been programmed.

Envisage positive outcomes

If you do as many people habitually do, and focus primarily on what you fear, or what you *don't* want to happen in your life, you will be programming your subconscious mind to believe that these outcomes are important to you, and due to the SGS, you will subsequently find yourself noticing all manner of things relating to that outcome. If, on the other hand you deliberately imagine the outcomes you do want to happen, you will be programming your subconscious mind to believe that this is what is important. You will find yourself noticing things that can expedite these outcomes.

Most people seem more inclined to imagine the outcomes they don't want to happen than those they do want to happen. Here is a technique for counteracting that tendency: On a piece of paper, list in a column, all the things you don't want to happen in your life; all the outcomes that you are worried may happen. Then look at each, and to its right, in an adjacent column, write the opposite outcome. Then make a point of staying focused on the items in the right-hand column instead of those on the left. Then notice the wonderful changes that happen in your life!

Miraculous effects

Sometimes, the powers of the subconscious mind seem miraculous, as if it has some way of influencing others as well as ourselves. One explanation is that we are not individual intelligences in isolation but are all interconnected on a subconscious level because communication is going on all the time between individuals, consciously as well as subconsciously, via many different channels. Joseph Murphy, author of *The Power of Your Subconscious Mind* refers to a 'universal subconscious mind' that connects all human beings, and possibly even all life forms.

Psychologist Albert Mehrabian concluded in the 1960s that only a small percentage of interpersonal communication is conscious. The vast majority of it happens subliminally through body language, intonation and other subtle means. Who knows what degree of communication goes on below the level of conscious perception? There is good evidence that long-distance telepathic communication occurs. Many scientists believe that thought forms can travel over distances rather like radio waves (which, of course, the average person cannot consciously detect through normal sensory perception). Many animals are known to have heightened levels of perception, to the extent that they can be aware of their owners' brain waves over long distances, and know when they are about to arrive home or when they are in peril. Many humans also seem able to detect such long-distance signaling.

Learn more about autosuggestion

Self-hypnosis and autosuggestion are both forms of self-programming. You might wish to develop your repertoire of self-programming techniques by reading more about self-hypnosis and autosuggestion. You can also obtain hypnosis recordings. If you can find ones that fit your requirements, you may want to try playing the recording while you are in bed, ready to sleep. But remember that insufficient repetition is likely to yield poor results.

RECOMMENDED ACTION STEPS

1) Buy a pack of 50 small blank cards and write a positive affirmation on each one. Place your cards in a place where you frequently spend idle time. Perhaps at your bedside, or near the kettle if you often linger there waiting for it to boil. It is best not to leave these cards anywhere where they will be seen by anyone who does not support your ideas and ambitions 100%. Read through these cards regularly. Make a habit of it. Revise the affirmations regularly, whenever it seems appropriate.

2) Get into the habit of repeating your most important affirmation every time you ascend a flight of stairs. What is the easiest way to get into that habit? Why, through self-programming of course! Imagine yourself doing it, in advance, and then you will find you remember to do it.

3) Consider experimenting with hypnosis recordings to reprogram yourself in the ways you desire. A good time to play such recordings is while you are in bed at night and when you first awaken in the morning.

11
CREATIVE THINKING
BE A GOLDMINE OF WINNING IDEAS

❖ *There is no doubt that creativity is the most important human resource of all. Without creativity, there would be no progress, and we would be forever repeating the same patterns.—Edward de Bono*

This chapter looks at the importance and value of being able to think creatively. It offers you techniques for becoming a master creative thinker. The ability to come up with exciting new ideas is a primary key to success. The ability to think creatively opens doors to new possibilities, and new opportunities. Creative ideas can solve stubborn problems, create wealth and improve the quality of your life in unlimited ways.

What typical qualities do creative thinkers have? They are often people who are constantly absorbing new knowledge on a wide range of human interests. They subconsciously find ways of applying a solution from one sphere of interest to solve a problem in a totally different sphere. They also practice. They often have the habit of spending time solving puzzles—ones that really stretch the intellect and force the mind to look for new, less obvious approaches.

A new way of thinking

The traditional styles of logical thinking tend to be ill-suited to producing innovative ideas. The old styles tend to be shallow and limited in scope. When solution-seeking in the traditional style, we tend to get locked into old pathways of search. Blinkers firmly in place, we often miss new possibilities and solutions.

It is possible to learn new styles of thinking, more suited to producing creative solutions. Whatever style we adopt, there is one factor that will certainly help us produce the solution we need, and that is a feeling of certainty that a practical solution *does* exist, and that it's simply a matter of finding it. Let's look at some new styles of creative thinking.

The drift-net technique

Think of the mind as an ocean, and the ideas swimming around therein as fish. Some will suit our needs and some won't. The old style of solution-seeking is rather like fishing with a rod. Each time a fish is caught, it is examined for suitability. If not suitable, it is cast back into the water, and the line is cast again.

There's a more effective method of fishing for ideas. Instead of using a fishing rod, you use a drift-net! The drift-net embraces a much wider volume of 'water', and catches a much greater number of fish that can be rapidly sorted. This is akin to 'lateral thinking' as expounded by Edward De Bono.

Creative thinkers seem to know how to gain access to a much greater number of potential solutions, and seem able to reach deeper into the hidden depths of the subconscious mind. To do this, it is necessary to be able to silence the chatter of the intellect, and all conscious logic-thinking, temporarily. Drift-net thinkers have the knack of sifting through vast numbers of potential solutions very rapidly. Their subconscious strategy seems to be to concentrate on quantity rather than quality, because there is then a greater chance of finding an effective solution. At the same time, there is more chance of hitting upon an idea that will trigger a line of thought that will produce a solution.

To master this art, it is also necessary to develop the ability to scan much vaster quantities of data, on a shallow level, so that each idea is checked for validity at lightning speed, and instantly released so that consecutive ideas may be examined in the same way. It is rather like speed-reading, except that one doesn't have to remember what has gone before—one only needs to take in what next comes into view. Focus is essential. One needs to go within, oblivious to distractions.

Here's another analogy: Imagine yourself searching for a lost wedding ring on someone's lawn. The traditional approach is to walk along looking carefully along the narrow band of grass in your path. Using the drift-net approach, you scan a much wider band of grass, opening up your receptivity; never letting your attention settle on any one spot, unless you think you've found something. You empty your head of all conscious thinking, so your thoughts don't distract you at the vital moment. By widening your scope of view just beyond that of the physical senses, you bring into play your subconscious faculties, which can quickly draw to you the lost object, or the elusive solution. Practice this technique and you will become proficient.

Group brainstorming

A group of people concentrating on a single problem together can be a powerful way of producing creative solutions. Brainstorming is similar to drift-netting, but each new idea that a group member puts forward is usually triggered or inspired by the previous idea. Ideas are thrown in at random by the group members in quick succession, until suitable ideas are produced. The secret of success is to do everything you can to reduce tension and inhibitions beforehand.

Making connections

A related technique for coming up with creative ideas is to 'force' the mind to find a connection between two seemingly unrelated ideas. Here's an exercise you can use to develop your ability to think creatively: Think of a problem you'd like to solve—preferably something that has had you baffled for some time. Now think of a number between one and a hundred. Write it down, then think of another number between one and ten. Now take a dictionary, and open it at the same page number as the first number you thought of.

Now look at the second number you thought of. If say, it was seven, you count down to the seventh word on the page. Your task now is to try using the drift-net technique to find a way of connecting that word with the problem so that a possible solution is suggested. It may seem utterly impossible, but don't let yourself off the hook so easily. Be certain that there is a connection. It is simply a matter of finding it. If not, then simply repeat the exercise until a solution emerges.

Get whacked!

Roger Von Oech published a book called *A Whack on the Side of the Head.* It is a book of innovation boosters to invoke and increase one's creativity. It's about making new connections to come up with fresh ideas. Also available is the *Creative Whack Pack*, a deck of cards, each conveying one of the innovation-invoking ploys from the book.

Use an oracle... in a special way

People usually associate oracles with superstition. However there is definitely a place for the oracle in the success-seeker's tool-box—*if used in a special way...*

There are many kinds of oracle: cards, dice, runes, pendulums, etc. The traditional way of using an oracle (the superstitious way) is to use it to attempt to predict the future. The adept achiever will rarely waste time on attempting to foretell the future using superstitious methods. However, he may well use oracles in a very different way. Apart from making light-hearted predictions, some oracles are ideally suited to gaining insights on problems, and finding new approaches to solving them. For thousands of years, the Chinese have been using an oracle designed specifically for this use.

The I-Ching

This ancient Chinese book contains sixty-four different explanations or answers to any question you care to ask it. The user focuses on the problem at hand and formulates a question concerning the problem, and then uses a random number-producing system to select one of the answers, or 'hexagrams' as they are called.

This still sounds rather like superstition, but the I-Ching is more sophisticated than that. Its sixty-four hexagrams are messages that are not always easy to interpret. You will often find yourself challenged to look at your problem from a different angle. It opens your mind to new approaches, ideas or understandings. It often prompts you to look at your deeper underlying motives and values. It often gives you insight into the deeper underlying causes of your situation.

Get a creative hobby

If you don't have a creative hobby already, then seriously think about adopting one. A creative hobby has a magical effect on one's general outlook and one's general creative abilities. You will find your mindset shifting into a permanent creative mode. The spin-off is that you will very likely become more creative in all aspects of your life - and that can only be a good thing.

Creativity and positivity go hand in hand; it is nearly impossible to be effectively creative unless your attitude is positive. Art, including painting, sculpting, photography, musicianship, writing fiction and poetry, jewellery-making, creative weaving, pottery and anything else involving design will nourish and expand your general level of creativity.

You will probably find that in your immediate area there are many groups that focus on some creative hobby. Consider joining one. Interacting with others who share the same hobby can open up a whole new world of discovery for you. The fringe benefit is that one of the surest ways to make new friends is through meeting people who pursue the same hobby that you've chosen. You will be surprised how your increased creativity and positivity will magnetize you and make you more interesting and appealing to others.

Eureka moments on awakening

Like many other people, I find that I get my best and most useful creative ideas while I am in the process of waking up after a night's sleep. There is something about that alpha-brainwave state that has a magical propensity for settling on viable solutions to dilemmas that have been simmering away in the subconscious mind. I find that the best way to increase the likelihood that a groundbreaking 'eureka moment' will occur at this time, is to focus on the issue in question when you are ready to go to sleep, the night before. It helps greatly if you are intensely concerned about the issue, because strong emotion is one of the keys to goading the subconscious mind into coming up with solutions.

❖ *Creative thinking is simply finding new, improved ways to do anything.---David J. Schwartz, Ph.D.*

❖ *Creativity is intelligence having fun.---Albert Einstein*

❖ *Genius means little more than the faculty of perceiving in an unhabitual way.*—William James

RECOMMENDED ACTION STEPS

1) Take up some form or creative pastime that you enjoy and spend more time doing that, and less time in mental free-fall watching television etc.

2) Get a copy of the I-Ching and learn to apply it as a problem-solving tool as described in this chapter.

3) Develop you brainstorming skills.

4) Focus on your challenges and dilemmas last thing at night, with strong emotion to encourage your subconscious mind to deliver viable solutions as you are in the process of awakening, the following morning.

12
CONTROLLED RELAXATION
FOR MULTIPLIED CAPABILITY

❖ *Nothing gives a person so much advantage over another as to remain always cool and unruffled under all circumstances. —Thomas Jefferson*

One of the special keys to extended capability is the learned ability to relax at will, even in the face of pressure. The ability to let go of things that do not benefit us is a key component of maturity. Without this skill, the affects of stress soon take their toll and render us depleted, burned out or defeated. In this chapter we'll learn a powerful technique for restoring cool, calm collectiveness in the face of pressure and adversity.

Some of the most accomplished people in history were renowned for their ability to stay calm regardless of the intensity of the situation. No-one can think optimally when flustered. When a person is in a panic he becomes ineffective and his decisions are likely to be ill-considered. One of the key skills of the winner is the ability to stay calm, relaxed and focused.

Accumulated tension

Accumulated tension, from everyday frustrations, dilemmas and irritations are bound to be a drain on one's energies. We can keep this under control through conscious and deliberate deep relaxation, practiced regularly, on the fly. And let's face it daily life is full of frustrations, dilemmas and irritations.

(Life is full of frustrations and dilemmas!)

Mindfulness is key

Present-centered awareness in the here and now, accompanied by a conscious awareness of one's breathing and an intention to keep it sufficiently deep and relaxed, is key to staying calm, come what may.

All thinking produces some physical tension. Pure concentration—awareness of the here and now—is one of the few mental modes that can be virtually tension-free. We become more tense and anxious when we stray from the present and fret about what could happen, or by wasting too much attention on what did happen.

The ability to relax at will

The exercise that follows has multiple benefits. The main one is that it teaches you to remain focused in the here and now, while remaining calm and relaxed. This skill, when mastered, is one of the most powerful success skills you can acquire. It also develops your power of will and your ability to direct your life.

Before we proceed, there are a few things we need to consider: Muscular movement and tension originate in the brain and are produced by *motor neuron activity*, of which there are two kinds: The first is directed by our will, and the second goes on automatically, even when we are asleep. The first kind is that which makes your hand move when you decide to reach for your glass of Hine 250 Cognac or your packet of Pork Scratchings. The second kind is that which causes your heart to keep beating, and which keeps you breathing throughout your sleeping hours. It is the first kind that needs to be subdued into almost complete inactivity in order to achieve complete relaxation and inner peace. The second, autonomic kind keeps operating as normal—or better than normal, unimpaired by interference from intellectual and emotional activity.

A suitable environment

It helps to practice deep relaxation in a place where you will be undisturbed for 30 minutes or more. Ideally, you want somewhere clean and quiet with no cold draughts or distracting noises. You need a firm, level surface to lie on, such as a floor. A soft bed is not suitable, as it may induce drowsiness. A thick, clean rug or exercise mat on the floor is ideal. Lie on your back, and place something under your head, but make it something fairly thin and firm, like a folded-up bath towel. A thick pillow or cushion is not suitable. If your head is inclined too much, you will not be able to relax fully without your throat and its air passage becoming constricted.

Loosen your clothing and lie in position. Open your legs slightly, and rest your arms by your sides (not on your chest or stomach, as this will impair your natural breathing). Wriggle around a little, until you are perfectly comfortable, and your body is lying perfectly straight. Some people prefer to lie from north to south, believing that this aligns their bodies with the earth's magnetic field. Experiment to see what works best for you.

The technique

So, let us proceed to relax and still the mind. Bring your full attention into the present moment—the here and now. Become aware of your entire body and at the same time, of any thoughts that enter your mind. Your aim is to keep your thoughts to the absolute minimum. They should become almost non-existent. We want to replace intellectual thinking with awareness. The only thoughts you have should hardly be thoughts at all, but merely the subtle activity of your will, vigilantly but gently guiding your mind to stay centered in the here and now throughout the session. Relax your entire body gently and continuously. Focus your awareness steadily on your body, becoming aware of all unnecessary tensions which can be released in an ongoing way. Be aware of your breathing. Release all control and let it become natural, smooth and effortless. We want to hand over control of our breathing to the autonomic nervous system. Do this by continuing to allow every muscle in your body to relax completely. (The key word here is 'allow'.) You may think this will cause you to stop breathing. Have no fear; you will not, except perhaps momentarily. There is an automatic reflex action built into the autonomic nervous system that makes you breathe in whenever the need becomes great enough.

So keep totally relaxed until your autonomic nervous system is taking care of your breathing in its own perfectly easy, energy-efficient way which is exactly the way that is most beneficial, healing and recuperative for the body at large. When you succeed in this, you will find yourself slipping into a profoundly more relaxed and peaceful state, as you start to enjoy the deeply regenerative state of effortless being. The benefits are many for the mind/body and its various internal systems, as they become naturally harmonized. Throughout the exercise, your prime goal is to keep your mind still, focused on the here and now, while relaxing and releasing bodily tensions, including those subtle cranial tensions which are thoughts. Ultimately, the goal is to be fully aware but free from thoughts. All thoughts produce hormonal excretions which disrupt our ability to completely relax.

The benefits

Some people get remarkable mental insights during these relaxation sessions. It's as though the stillness of the mind allows a new channel to the subconscious mind to open up. These flashes of inspiration are never consciously produced; they only appear when the mind is close to stillness. If this happens to you, you can either stop the session and take action according to the inspiration you've received, or you can look upon it as just another thought trying to tempt your mind into activity again. You might consider ignoring these flashes of inspiration unless they are particularly exciting, or make a note of them and continue with the exercise.

If you attempt this technique when you are tired and in need of sleep, you may fall asleep during the session. If you find yourself drifting off when you know you don't need sleep, it may be that you are not relaxing properly. Try intensifying your resolve to relax and your sleepiness may disappear. If not, it simply means that your body really does need sleep. In that case, go and sleep and continue after you wake up.

If you can find somewhere to practice during the day, perhaps in your lunch break, you should find that your performance improves dramatically. The benefits of proper and complete relaxation should not be underestimated. Illnesses can be cured by this technique alone; not just mental maladies like depression, but even physical illnesses. The medical profession is beginning to realize that many more illnesses originate in the mind than was previously believed. This technique, when performed diligently, will banish any illness-producing thought patterns from the mind. At the same time, the increased calmness of the system enables the immune system to work more effectively.

Perhaps the main benefits you will gain are an increased capacity to concentrate effectively, greater willpower and a calmer, more intelligent mind. The ability to concentrate effectively is one of the most important success skills of all. By improving your concentration, you gain greater power to think things through, and logically predict future events. You will also increase your capacity to follow other people's thinking. Thus, your ability to learn will increase, and your relationships will improve.

Life-saving benefits

Did you see the movie called Adrift (2006), directed by Hans Horn? It was about a group of men and women who went sailing on a large ketch, off the coast of Mexico. A couple of days into their excursion, they were all soaking up the sun on deck amid very calm waters, while the boat was not under sail. After a few drinks, they decided to enjoy a swim. They all dived overboard, only to realize that the sides of the boat were a few feet too high, so that none of them could reach the boat's gunwales in order to pull themselves out of the water and back into the boat.

They spent many hours treading water, very fearful of their perilous situation, unable to find any way of getting back on board. Three of the party eventually drowned, leaving just two out of five.

One of them eventually had a brainwave. He removed the clear plastic from his diving goggles. It was a single piece of clear plastic to accommodate both eyes, rather than the type with a separate glass for each eye. There was a door in the side of the yacht which could only be opened from on board. He managed to jam the piece of clear plastic into the crack between the door and the hull. While he hung on to this, the other remaining survivor was just able to climb onto his shoulders, and, after several attempts manage to reach up to the gunwale and climb aboard.

After watching this gripping movie, it occurred to me that this story could be considered a poignant fable. It reminded me that so many times, when we find ourselves in a seemingly desperate situation we may think we have no way out, but more often than not, there *is* a way out of the predicament, if only we could see it. I have been given certain puzzles to solve that seemed utterly impossible—until someone showed me the secret.

When the going gets really desperate, we often find ourselves gaining access to remarkable reserves of mind power, just long enough for a solution to emerge. That is, provided we don't panic.

In cases where we are not quite scared enough to get that merciful access to those mental reserves, we have to look for other ways to gain access to our latent mental powerhouse.

Hope, faith, optimism

It has been noted that we are more likely to find the solution to a crisis or emergency, if we have the optimism to believe that a solution probably exists, if we can but deduce it. This may be quite a reasonable assumption when we consider the incredible latent powers of the human mind. Everything we have ever experienced has been fed into our subconscious mind. That is an awesome amount of raw material for our human supercomputer to work with.

How many times have you thought to yourself (some time after the event): "Why didn't I think of that? It's so obvious!" From my own experience, more often than not, a solution occurs to me later. Sometimes years later, admittedly... but the point is that the solution was there and it could have occurred to me if I had just thought about the situation in the right way. So what is the right way? Well, that clearly varies, according to the situation and the person involved. What is much clearer is what the least effective way is. Panicking is definitely not conducive to effective problem solving. Nor is pessimism. If you assume that there is no solution, you are not going to bother to look for one!

Maintaining hope is vital because hope, intelligence and mental alacrity go hand in hand. Having faith in the power of logical reasoning often pays off more than anything else in some situations. Whenever I have mislaid my keys or cell phone, I have found that I can hunt for hours and end up as clueless as I was at the outset. Conversely, when I give up hunting like a headless chicken and sit down and focus internally with pure cold logic on all known facts leading up to the loss, the answer usually comes to light. Once you start feeding real known facts into the cranial computer, it becomes possible for it to generate logical solutions.

Until we discover quicker and better techniques for gaining instant access to the awesome power of logic and our subconscious human computer with its vast data-banks, the best advice we have seems to be: (1) to have faith that a solution exists, provided we think clearly and logically and take enough care not to overlook anything; (2) to think logically, based on the known facts; (3) to stay as cool, calm and collected as possible. Deep breathing can help here.

As a rule there are usually many more avenues of exploration that we could pursue, that don't occur to us when in the midst of a fearful situation. Would it be too far-fetched to propose that there is a solution to almost every problem, if only we could think of it? The occasions when we cannot find one are usually those times when we resign ourselves to defeatism or become otherwise locked into one-track thinking.

What struck me about the *Adrift* story, was that the group-member who eventually came up with the solution to their bleak predicament, was the one who stayed calm and quietly focused without succumbing to panic. The saying "empty vessels make the most noise" carries credence. The mind is just not very effective when it is full of noise, and a panicking mind is a noisy mind indeed.

In the *Adrift* story, the party member who gave up and drowned was the one who was unfortunate enough to be the most susceptible to morbid defeatism, which is closely related to panic. There was no physical reason why she could not have survived until the solution was found.

❖ *The more tranquil a man becomes, the greater is his success, his influence, his power for good. Calmness of mind is one of the beautiful jewels of wisdom.—James Allen*

❖ *When I struggle and try to organize the Atlantic to my specifications, I sink. If I flail and thrash and growl and grumble, I go under. But, if I let go and float, I am borne aloft.—Marie Stilkind*

❖ *One cool judgment is worth a thousand hasty counsels. The thing to do is to supply light and not heat.*
  —Woodrow T. Wilson

❖ *The world belongs to the enthusiast who keeps cool.*
  —William Mcfee

❖ *Stress is an ignorant state. It believes that everything is an emergency.—Natalie Goldberg*

❖ *The greatest weapon against stress is our ability to choose one thought over another.—William James*

❖ *The more tranquil a man becomes, the greater is his success, his influence, his power for good. Calmness of mind is one of the beautiful jewels of wisdom.—James Allen*

❖ *A samurai must remain calm at all times even in the face of danger.—Chris Bradford*

RECOMMENDED ACTION STEPS

1) Allocate a quiet place in your home for regular deep relaxation practice. Practice daily—or whenever you feel the stresses of life are adversely affecting you.

2) Lie down or sit back when you are free from distractions, and cast your mind back to some seemingly impossible predicament you have experienced in the past. If you were transported back to that situation now, how would you approach it differently? Imagine how you would approach it if something similar happens in future.

13
CONCENTRATION POWER
AND ITS DYNAMIC POTENTIAL

❖ *Concentration is the master key to all success. It is the fundamental law of achievement.* —Orison Swett Marden

Great things can be achieved through the power of full focus and concentration. In this chapter we consider the tremendous power of concentration. We look at ways to increase this essential skill for unleashing our latent potential to move us towards the achievement of major goals and objectives.

Meditation and concentration practice have amazing benefits for mental and physical health, wellbeing and personal fulfillment.

There is a great deal of misunderstanding about meditation and what it is. The type of meditation we are going to touch on in this chapter, is the kind that holds the most benefits and the greatest potential to raise intelligence and improve health and longevity.

Misunderstandings about meditation

The word 'meditation' is bandied about in today's world, with meanings ranging from 'guided meditation' to mantra repetition to idle reflection and contemplation. There seems to be a great deal of confusion and misunderstanding about the difference between contemplation, concentration and meditation. The world's most advanced schools of mental self-development regard these as three progressive stages or states on the path to total self mastery. Let's look at each in turn:

1) Contemplation

The first stage, contemplation, is an increased state of mental focus, where one follows a specific train of thought about some subject or object. The well-known 'guided meditation' (actually not meditation at all) is a case in point. Contemplation is something that most people can achieve and benefit from without any extensive training.

2) Concentration

Concentration (in the context of mental science) is a step further. This is less easy to achieve, and takes practice.

Its aim is to bring the awareness unwaveringly into the present, with no glancing forwards or backwards in time. This is usually aided by focusing the attention unwaveringly on some object such as a candle flame. Alternatively one might focus on some sensation in the body such as that of the air entering and leaving the nostrils. In order to achieve this unwavering focus, it is necessary to subdue all intellectual activity, because thought is not our chosen object of focus. Again, many people refer to this as 'meditation' but it actually falls short of true meditation, which is the next stage.

3) Meditation

The next stage (true meditation) is the most difficult to achieve. The thinking part of our mind (our intellect) has been likened to a monkey or a wild horse that is difficult to tame. However, it can be tamed through concentration and meditation, if such practices are carried out alone with as little distraction as possible. Anyone who advocates or promotes repetitive group meditation as the best way to progress should be regarded with cynicism and skepticism. There are plenty of groups and organizations out there that are really cults. They need your money to pay their teachers and like so many religious organizations, worldwide, use mind-control techniques (a form of hypnosis) to dupe people into believing they are the true and only path to... whatever. Furthermore, what they call 'meditation' is invariably either contemplation or concentration at best. They attempt to make meditation more appealing by turning it into a social activity, which is misleading nonsense.

Swami Vivekananda, one of the great Yogic masters of the last century, touches on these mind control techniques in his commentaries: "Think of the mind as a team of wild horses, and rather than controlling them through self control, full focus and taking hold of the reins, you ask another to hit them on the head to stun them into a submissive state for a short period of time. Each time another stuns the horses into submission, you lose some of your own mental energy. From continued regular sessions of hypnosis from another person, entering into this docile state, instead of gaining power and better control, the mind can become a shapeless powerless mass eventually leading to the mental asylum."

The true mental masters throughout history – including those whose achievements left the greatest mark on humanity – meditated in solitude; Jesus and Siddhartha Gautama (Buddha) being arguably the cream of the crop, finding their own way to higher knowledge through intuition rather than indoctrination from some religious or metaphysical cult. The higher inspiration that is the real jewel in the centre of the lotus, so to speak, is found and awakened within, without any form of conditioning or indoctrination from without. For that very reason, I am not going to presume to instruct you in these matters. Buy practicing the preliminary two stages of contemplation and concentration and assimilating your own discoveries and revelations, you will hopefully find your own way to the higher levels of the mind—your own true connection with Higher Intelligence, whose potential power and insight is limitless.

The choice is yours

Whether you wish to attain the levels of mental mastery associated with the above-mentioned masters is up to you. You may wish to limit yourself to concentration practice, which in itself has profound benefits in the field of self-mastery and the elevation of intelligence.

Effective concentration is a key to higher achievement in all fields of successful living, personal power, and the enjoyment of life.

A capable, intelligent mind has a greater ability to succeed. The more effectively you can analyze a situation, plan a detailed course of action and solve problems along the way, the more successful you will be. The main element in these skills is not intellectual knowledge, but the ability to concentrate—to direct and sustain a train of logic to its natural conclusion. You'll find many an intellectual who has failed to become successful, and you'll find many people who lack formal education who have achieved great success. These are people who have developed their own talents through sustained, focused attention.

Concentration results in better performance

The ability to concentrate effectively with sustained unwavering attention is the magic ingredient that enhances mental and physical dexterity. With concentration, almost miraculous things are achieved. Concentration is what enables some people to multiply two 8-digit numbers together mentally and come up with the correct answer, or cross the Niagara Falls on a tightrope, or become the world snooker champion. It's what enabled Mozart to compose entire pages of full-score symphonic music in his head and then write it all down in musical notation without needing to make a single correction.

Concentration brings more effective learning

Those who do well in schools are those who are able to direct and sustain focused attention. Being able to concentrate enables one to follow a train of thought, and in the learning process we need to follow the train of thought of our teacher as far as possible. If our attention wanders onto irrelevant thoughts, we may lose the thread. We can attempt to get back into the teacher's train of thought, but by this time we are often too late; proper comprehension of the subject has been disrupted.

Success through clear thinking

When planning, problem-solving, and analyzing information, we have to use concentration to direct and follow our own train of thought. If concentration fails and our mind wanders, our thinking becomes blurred, diffused and confused. People who are considered intelligent are those who can concentrate well and think logically. Logic is a very basic intellectual ability which most people understand instinctively. Concentration, on the other hand, is a skill.

Personal interest improves concentration

We concentrate most effectively when we are interested in the subject. Unfortunately not all of life is interesting, and to be a high achiever one needs to be able to concentrate on subjects that are difficult, dull or otherwise unpleasant. We must have some interest to be able to concentrate at all, but our interest may be more in the long-term goals that the study of the subject will help achieve, rather than in the subject itself. In these circumstances, concentration does not come naturally to most people. They have to sustain an effort to keep their attention from wandering.

By developing your concentration skills, you will find it much easier to pay attention to both tedious and interesting matters. This is one of the most important skills necessary for becoming more successful in life. There's a good argument for saying that it should be one of the first skills every young child should learn. If this were the case, there would surely be a far higher success rate in schools and colleges, and beyond, in the commercial world as well as in the field of human relations.

Success through planning

Armed with the ability to concentrate better, you'll be better equipped to make the necessary plans that will lead you step by step to your chosen goals. Concentration enables clear, detailed thinking, and therefore effective planning.

Success through problem-solving

Life is fraught with problems and obstacles. With effective concentration, we can think problems through, clearly and logically, devising solutions and mentally testing them before putting them into action.

Success through analyzing information

The other type of thinking that brings success is the ability to analyze information and situations; in other words, figuring things out for yourself. Much of what we learn is not easy to understand; we need to look at the information mentally, and digest it, rather as a computer would. When it all clicks into place, we have reached understanding. Better concentration improves this process.

Heightened enjoyment

Finally, what is success if it doesn't involve some kind of enjoyment? What is a successful person if he cannot experience pleasure? Concentration heightens pleasure. When the attention is undivided, one can savor moments of pleasure with greater intensity and satisfaction. To the person who cannot concentrate, all pleasure is fleeting. This leads to an insatiable desire for more and more of the pleasure-giving thing. People with poor concentration are thus prone to addictions and over-indulgence.

Social success

A major element of personal success is success in relationships. Successful relationships rely on good communication and good understanding. Both improve with concentration. To understand someone, you have to be able to follow his or her trains of thought. Clear analysis leads to understanding. Effective concentration helps the process. And you can communicate your ideas better if you can formulate your thinking clearly and communicate it clearly through the power of good focus.

Developing concentration has spiraling benefits

Take for example, a successful musician who first developed his powers of concentration. His superior focus enables him to learn new pieces of music more effectively. His quick learning gives him confidence, which in turn leads to greater satisfaction, which in turn leads to even better concentration. This spiraling of benefits is the reward for developing your concentration. It applies to every kind of human pursuit. Conversely, poor concentration induces a vicious circle of failure.

```
        Poor                              Improved
    concentration                       concentration
   Poor                              Improved      Improved
 learning    Self-doubt           self-confidence   learning
   Poor      Distracting           Improved inner   Improved
performance    fears                 well-being    performance

 The Spiral of Failure              The Spiral of Success
```

Factors that can undermine concentration

Here are some of the main factors that make concentration difficult for most people. Try to eliminate them if you can before attempting full concentration.

Environmental distractions

The most obvious enemies of concentration are irritating noises, smells and distractions from people's conversation, television, radio, kids playing, dripping taps, draughts, neighbors' noise, dogs barking, etc. Uncomfortable room temperature, tight clothing, bodily aches and pains all distract. Untidy surroundings can also cause subconscious distraction.

The desire for quick gratification

This is another very common distraction—one that originates within. The distraction may be the desire to smoke a cigarette or make a cup of coffee. Alternatively, it may come in the form of associated thoughts which lure one's attention away from the true subject—thoughts which promise reward or pleasure but which are not relevant to the mental task in hand. These thoughts may be memories, reveries, or totally unrelated observations.

Worry

If there is some pressing problem in the back of your mind, you will find it hard to sustain concentration on your subject. Try to resolve the problem if you can. It is usually best to face your worries and deal with them head-on.

Emotions

Strained or broken relationships or the loss of a loved one, can result in unpleasant emotions and other distracting thoughts that can interfere with your ability to concentrate well. So make every effort to patch up and repair any floundering relationships.

Fatigue

The mind loses its ability to concentrate as it becomes tired. For this reason, you might plan your activities so that you carry out, early in the day, tasks requiring the most concentration.

Improving your concentration-power

Concentration is improved by learning to direct and sustain relaxed attention. 'Concentration' as a word can conjure up pictures of furrowed brows, tension and effort. But concentration is most effective when one is relaxed and calm, and this is the kind of concentration we seek. If you allow physical and nervous tension to creep in, you will tire yourself out prematurely.

Focusing on the task at hand while also paying attention to staying relaxed requires dividing one's attention. So we need an exercise that trains us to do both things together. The following method of mental practice is optimal for the kind of results we are looking for. It comprises the first two stages of what we have already mentioned: the first two stages of the trifold path to ultimate self-mastery. In this form, it will also prepare you for the third and ultimate stage (meditation itself) should you wish to progress further. Before you begin, find a place where you won't be disturbed.

The method

The following guidance assumes that you have no physical injury or deformity that makes it unsuitable for you. Ideally, sit on low chair (the lower the better), with your lower legs (calves and shins) crossed in such a way that you can keep your spine erect, perfectly balanced, with as little effort as possible. Even better, if you are physically able, sit cross-legged on the floor, or if that is too uncomfortable, perhaps you can sit cross-legged with one or more pillows under your buttocks. Rest your hands in as relaxed a way as possible, on your thighs or in your lap. Close your eyes and direct your attention to releasing all unnecessary tension from your body while keeping the spine erect. Let your eyes relax. Stay steadily focused on releasing all unnecessary tensions and emotions from your system. Sustain your relaxed focus on this task, allowing your breathing to become as easy, smooth, natural and effortless as possible. Your mind may tend to wander at first, but don't get frustrated; just bring your attention back on track. With practice, control of your attention will improve.

If you find that your attention is all over the place and hard to bring under control, start counting your breaths; count each out-breath from 1 to 4 and then repeat indefinitely. Alternatively, you can repeat a single word (mantra) in time with each out-breath. A word such as 'peace' makes sense, since this is after all what we are aiming for: complete peace at last, from the distraction of an untamed intellect.

Alternatively, you could focus on a candle flame. You should soon find that the chattering of the intellect begins to abate, and focused, calm attention can then prevail. When it does, you can direct your focus onto the sensation of your breath entering and leaving your nostrils. Focusing on the breath is good because the breath is an excellent signal of what is going on subconsciously. It reacts to adrenaline and other hormones which are triggered by mental activity conscious or subconscious (the stuff we seek to subdue and bring under control).

Once you are in a calmer state, a good thing to fully focus your attention on, is some abstract concept of the highest virtue, such a pure, all-encompassing love, or perhaps loving-kindness. You should find that this has a tremendously wholesome effect on your mental and bodily wellbeing, with very definite health benefits too.

Resistance to Meditating

When you start to meditate, you may find that distracting thoughts and feelings try to gate-crash your inner peace—that is, thoughts or feelings irrelevant to your chosen subject of focus. Some meditation teachers recommend that when this happens, it is best to acknowledge their existence but then gently guide your attention back onto the subject you have chosen to focus on.

The more you progress with this, the more you will notice your life and wellbeing improving in numerous ways.

Practice regularly. If you find it awkward to maintain an erect spine for long periods, practice for short periods at first—perhaps five to ten minutes. Stop if you feel any strain. It gets easier and more natural with practice. As time passes, you can comfortably increase the duration of the exercise to, say, twenty to thirty minutes or more. Ideally, you will sustain the exercise until you have released all unwanted mental and nervous tensions, and established a very calm, relaxed and comfortable state of body and mind.

You may consider placing a (preferably silent) clock within your field of vision that you can glance at occasionally, to see when your practice period is coming to an end.

Releasing persistent bodily tension

To release all unnecessary emotional, muscular and nervous tensions during your session, you can focus your attention on your entire body at once, and release all tensions simultaneously and continuously. This is also good concentration practice. Aim to retain only the minimum tension necessary to maintain your balanced erect posture.

Notice the benefits

During your normal daily activity, notice the subtle improvements in your demeanor and inner wellbeing, and continue this exercise twice every day, starting with ten minutes and progressing to longer sessions. The exact duration of each session is not critical. Listen to your body to gain insight into what feels right for you. Do not strain, and do not force yourself to remain awake if you feel that your body needs to sleep. Do these practice sessions at times of the day when you are not likely to become drowsy.

You may well find that these sessions improve your outlook in many ways and you may notice yourself becoming more resourceful and creative. Don't be disheartened by lack of detectible results, during or immediately after a session. It's not the evident results that count, but the degree to which you persist with the program and perform your sessions correctly with self-discipline. Be vigilant to a wandering mind and nip all such wanderings in the bud, gently bringing your attention back where it should be.

Sometimes you will experience instant benefits and new insights. On other occasions you may detect no benefits at all. The benefits are not always immediately obvious, but they are nevertheless acquired.

RECOMMENDED ACTION STEP

1) **Practice meditation regularly, following the above guidelines. Once or even twice daily would be ideal. To get into the habit, try using the techniques covered in the chapter on habits, rather than relying on willpower alone.**

2) **After each meditation session, write in your A-Log any new observations or insights, and any things you learned about your inner workings.**

14
EMOTIONAL MATURITY
& EMOTIONAL INTELLIGENCE

- *Age is just a number. Maturity is a choice.* —Harry Styles
- *Maturity is achieved when a person postpones immediate pleasures for long-term values.* —Joshua L. Liebman

In this chapter we explore the merits and value of emotional maturity. In any great endeavor or enterprise there will be times of difficulty, disappointment, conflict and even betrayal. It takes an emotionally mature person to weather the storm, accept what cannot be changed, and come through intact with an undiminished resolve, while preserving valuable relationships. Emotional maturity earns you the well-deserved respect of your own self and of others. It's a key to living optimally.

Many years ago, I heard someone propose a definition of the word 'maturity'. That definition was: *'having good control of one's emotions.'* When I ran this one through my internal 'does it stack up' filter, I realized it made good sense. To illustrate the viability of this definition, consider for a moment, the antithesis of maturity. That would be babyhood. What are the characteristics of the infantile personality? I think you'll agree that one key is the complete inability to control emotions. The baby cries its eyes out until there is not an ounce of grief left in its physiology. It throws temper tantrums with total abandon and it also laughs heartily, devoid of all self-consciousness. If we, as adults, behaved in this way, we would soon find ourselves under psychiatric care!

From an early age, with guidance from our guardians and teachers, along with contemptuous criticism from our peers and siblings, we learn ever-increasing control of our emotional reactions. We also increasingly discover the adverse consequences of not restraining our emotions during our passage through the University of Life.

By the time we reach adulthood, we have (hopefully) learned much about the advantages of emotional self-management. We learn how to avoid the inclination to fly into a rage when our boss pushes us too far, or when another driver cuts us off on the highway. We still have the same emotional makeup that we always had, but we accumulate a repertoire of techniques for keeping our emotional reactions in check so that we can operate effectively in the adult world, avoid alienating people and being fired from our jobs.

Besides getting us into trouble, unchecked emotional responses impede objective thinking and undermine our effectiveness as students, business people, employees, parents or whatever adult role we aspire to. People who have good control of their emotional states do better in life than those who don't. Good emotional self-control is one of the foremost qualities that employers look for when evaluating employees. It's one of the most important qualities that partner-seekers look for. Lack of emotional control is one of the topmost reasons that employees lose their jobs and partners fall out. It's also why people find themselves washed up on the rocks of depression, terminal bitterness and worse.

Emotions do have value

Emotional maturity is not about being completely devoid of emotion. Such traits are reserved for Dr Spock, his fellow Vulcans and other fictional characters. However, it's very interesting to note how so many real-world females drool over Dr Spock! Someone conducted research into why this was so, and found it was exactly because he resembled a human who had developed full control of his emotional responses – the epitome of emotional maturity.

People who have great levels of emotional maturity still experience occasional grief, sadness and frustration. It would be hard to imagine how there could be any joy in life without there being an opposite. Emotions do have value. Uncomfortable feelings and emotions can be valuable calls to action. And of course human love in its various forms is one of the primary sweeteners of life. And love of life itself is one of the most valuable attitudes we can develop.

❖ *Feelings are much like waves, we can't stop them from coming but we can choose which one to surf.*
—Jonatan Mårtensson

Apart from streamlining our life skills and success potential, there is another reason why emotional maturity becomes increasingly important as we grow older: The older we get, the more traumas of various kinds can become more frequent. Parents, friends and loved ones increasingly seem to drop like flies around us usually at some point after mid-life. And the older we get, the more we have to contend with dwindling energy, health issues and ultimately, our own death. Hopefully, by the time that day arrives, we will have learned emotional coping techniques to the extent that we can handle it.

But let's not wait until that day before we are forced into full maturity! The earlier we can achieve emotional maturity, the more of our life we can spend getting ahead and achieving our dreams without unmanaged emotions tripping us up at every turn in the road like snakes in a game of snakes and ladders.

Man, know thyself!

Those words (or words to that effect) were carved in the forecourt of the Temple of Apollo at Delphi in ancient Greece, according to the Greek writer Pausanias. If so, the philosophical ancient Greeks must have considered this advice to be of paramount importance. And of course, ancient Greece is considered the cradle of Western civilisation, and the most civilized and socially advanced society of the ancient world. Perhaps that's in part because they followed the above advice. Let us consider what was meant by those wise words.

Self-knowledge and self-awareness is key

Self-awareness is the cornerstone of developing emotional maturity. That is, knowing our own patterns of emotional responses and how those responses benefit or hinder our effectiveness in life. Equally, it pays to notice how our emotions manifest themselves in our behavior and thinking. It pays to get into the habit of self-observation, noticing the physical manifestation of our emotions through bodily sensations. It pays to notice patterns in our behavioral responses to emotions that we have exhibited repeatedly, and constantly seek ways to improve how we manage our emotions and how we react to them. Are your habitual responses bringing optimal results for you or are they causing you problems? If so, consider ways you would prefer to react and behave. Consider new ways of managing your emotions. Pay attention to how other people manage theirs. Can you learn from them and adopt or adapt their techniques?

Practice deciding how to react to emotions

When you notice emotional responses that don't serve your best interests, think of how you want to react differently. Imagine alternative approaches that would better serve your interests - then put them into practice.

When misfortune besets you, it is okay to immerse yourself in an inevitable wave of emotion - but don't let that wave hijack your soul and drag you down permanently. Once the initial wave has passed, decide how you want to handle successive waves. Then practice handling them in that way. This is essence of emotional maturity.

Avoid self-condemnation

Remember; emotions are natural, so acknowledge them and avoid judging or condemning yourself for your emotions, but be open to new ways of managing those emotions and feelings so that they don't get you into trouble or get in the way of your goals and objectives.

Learn to change your state at will

Just as we can become aware of things that trigger unwanted emotional states, we can also become aware of the things that trigger good states, and learn to take advantage of them. You can learn to induce optimism, goodwill and other beneficial emotional states by making use of these triggers. Does certain music do it for you? Or perhaps casting your mind back to some good memory or a change of attire or surroundings works for you. Whatever works for you, take advantage of it, because we are so much more effective when our internal emotional environment is harmonious.

Learn to 'break state' in others too

Emotions are infectious. Psychologists talk about emotional contagion. One only has to watch the mob mentality during riots and at rock concerts to see it in action. We are all susceptible to being affected by other people's mindsets and emotional states, so it pays to learn to change other people's states as well as our own. One of the most effective techniques is humor. It can short-cut the voids in human empathy in an instant, when used with finesse. Some form of surprise is often effective at breaking people's states.

163

Of course, it is much easier to affect someone else's emotional state in a positive way if we are already in control of our own state, so it is generally wise to adopt the broad principle of seeking to change our own emotional state first before trying to affect others.

Learn from others

One of the most important steps to self-improvement is having an open mind and the willingness to consider new views and different standpoints. It pays to watch debates on television and in real life, in which skilled debaters discuss emotionally charged subjects. Notice the techniques these debaters use to stay cool and maintain their dignity. You can adopt and adapt their techniques for your own use. Talk to others who you recognize as having great emotional self-control and ask them about their approaches. I once asked someone how they managed to maintain perfect composure while enduring the most malicious face-to-face character assassination. The victim shared his approach with me. He said: "I never take the bait; I always take a deep breath and count from one to five and think of how my best self would react." That's a great technique to adopt.

Consider reading books and biographies about people who have made the most of grim situations that might well have destroyed other people. Useful techniques are all around us waiting to be noticed, collected and adopted. All it takes is awareness, an open mind and a desire to improve.

Timely control of emotions

Emotions are triggered by our subconscious mind in response to sensory input and our own thoughts and memories. The exact way the subconscious mind triggers emotions depends on how it has been programmed since the day we were born. A lot of that programming does not suit our best interests. Prior to around the age of ten or eleven, when our intellects were neither fully developed nor equipped with a mature sense of discernment, we tended to trustingly accept any programming that was foisted on us. It is prior to this age that most psychological and long-term emotional difficulties begin. However, it is reassuring to know that all adverse programming can be undone through conscious intention if we use effective techniques diligently. Our very characters are mostly the result of programming since birth. So it is possible to reprogram ourselves to become the kind of person we want to become. And that includes the ways our emotions are triggered by different situations and the way we respond to them. Creating a new you through reprogramming is something that's explored in greater depth in another chapter, and it's one of the most important and self-empowering topics covered in this book.

Lose your emotional baggage

Many emotions are a drain and a strain. It can be difficult to let go of intense emotions in the heat of the moment, but we can 'bite the bullet' until we are in a position to release or channel the emotions in beneficial ways. These may include physical exercise to burn off the unwanted hormones or practicing deep relaxation. Be careful to avoid escapism such as drug or alcohol abuse. Such methods are unhealthy and don't effectively change our underlying patterns. Daily meditation practice is a phenomenal way to improve one's overall state by naturally dissolving one's emotional baggage.

RECOMMENDED ACTION STEPS

1) Keep a note of how you react to things, emotionally. Take special note of ways you react that are not ideal.

2) Keep note of the new techniques you adopt for better managing your emotions and your emotional reactions

3) Watch TV debates on emotionally charged subjects. And observe how the participants you most admire manage their emotional reactions. Notice how they maintain their dignity.

4) Meditate daily, using the method described in this book.

5) Keep a record, in your A-Log of new techniques you can adopt or adapt as your own.

❖ *If a man empties his purse into his head no one can take it away from him. An investment in knowledge always pays the best interest. —Benjamin Franklin*

15
PLUG THOSE KNOWLEDGE GAPS
BEFORE THEY SINK YOU!

❖ *Ask a question and you're a fool for three minutes; do not ask a question and you're a fool for the rest of your life.*
 —Chinese Proverb

This chapter looks at the importance of being equipped with adequate knowledge of a suitable nature and quality to achieve your aims, whatever they may be. Whatever your ambition, it's imperative to know how to achieve it and with the least expense and effort. This chapter helps you to acquire that knowledge from the most cost-effective sources.

You may notice that you often recognize a gap in your knowledge – a gap that would benefit from being filled with the knowledge that would help you attain your goals and objectives efficiently. It could be anything from learning the meaning of a single word to acquiring advanced knowledge on some subject. Time judiciously invested in learning the most important things you need to know, can save hours, days, weeks or months of wasted time. Why spend months learning something from trial and error when you could have done it the best way possible from the start, if you had only taken the time to find out what others have learned from experience and research? It is so important to be vigilant about recognizing gaps in your knowledge that would benefit from being filled. Think of these gaps as holes in the side of your boat. Any one of them could result in the sinking of your boat and all it contains – so it really pays to keep your boat as watertight as possible, with the time available.

Gaining knowledge is so easy now

Knowledge is infinitely more accessible today than it ever was in the past, thanks to the Internet. The Internet offers us a boundless sea of information at little cost. All you need to do is type in a word or phrase to search for and you are immediately presented with a relevant list of articles, websites, video presentations and downloadable documents. The immense value of this resource is mind-boggling. It opens up a vastly enhanced potential for every one of us. Make sure you take full advantage of it. You can now study for a degree or diploma in almost any subject that interests you without even leaving your home if you so wish.

Key Internet sites

Certain websites excel for accessing the material you have determined you need to learn about. Particularly noteworthy at the time of writing, we have:

- Wikipedia (the ultimate online encyclopedia)
- Google (the most popular Internet search engine)
- YouTube (videos, from short to long, on all subjects)

Be selective and focus on key issues

Since time is of the essence to every success-oriented person, be selective when seeking suitable and valid sources and examples of the subject of enquiry. Beware that a lot of material on the Internet is designed primarily to make money for the person publishing it. The profit motive often takes precedence over the desire to offer quality information. Indeed, whole subjects have emerged backed up with lots of hype but with very little actual merit, purely because people can make money teaching them! A key skill is learning to sort the wheat from the chaff.

Also remember that a lot of poor-quality information has been posted on the internet by people who don't fully understand the subject of their writing. Such people are often motivated by a need to produce an essay, article, book or report for all sorts of reasons.

It is easy to fall into the trap of thinking that literature, from a few words to a whole book, is legitimate and credible simply because it is visually well-presented.

At the time of writing, Wikipedia is relatively reliable and free of commercial 'chaff', and can usually be relied on for factual and accurate information. With YouTube, while the audio-visual medium has wonderful advantages, you need to be more selective, because many of the videos are there primarily because the poster receives advertising revenues and other fringe benefits from posting videos there. The same detrimental effects of the profit motive also apply in some degree to the list of websites that your favorite search engine offers up at your bidding. However, thankfully, the searching systems used by Google and YouTube do have some degree of built-in selectivity, using sophisticated algorithms. However, they are far from infallible, so judicious discernment is still recommended.

Keep your goals in mind, constantly

When searching for the information you need on the Internet or anywhere else, there is always the allure of irrelevant material seeking to divert your attention, so make a sustained effort to keep focused on your goal. Keep asking yourself what is the key issue you need to find out at every given moment, and stay focused on that alone. Staying focused is one of the key traits of the high achiever.

Download key material to absorb later

There is only so much one can effectively absorb while sitting in front of a computer before eye strain and other discomforts start to take their toll. If you save the material to a CD, DVD, or memory stick, or print it out, you can study it later, while engaged in other activities that don't require your full attention. Have your printouts or suitable media player within easy reach so that you can relax and absorb the information at your leisure. There follows a list of possible learning opportunities:

- when you are in bed but not inclined to sleep,
- whenever there is nothing worth watching on TV
- when you go for a walk
- when you go on a journey
- when you are driving

If you don't have Internet access...

Most people, in the civilized world have Internet access nowadays. Anyone who doesn't is at a serious competitive disadvantage when it comes to learning.

If, for any reason, the Internet is not available to you, you can still look for other means of finding out what you need to know. Other resources could include:

- public libraries
- book shops
- citizens' advice bureaus
- conversations with people in-the-know

You can accelerate your book-learning massively by learning to speed-read. I particularly recommend Tony Buzan's excellent books on the subject, such as *The Speed Reading Book.*

Cultivate a passion for learning

Curiosity may have killed the cat, but a hunger for knowledge is what makes for a learned and wise person. Bear in mind that increasing one's knowledge requires effort and that is what discourages many people and keeps them in a state of relative ignorance. However, the more one learns, the easier learning becomes. However, be prepared to put some effort into your learning pursuits in order to get ahead.

- ❖ *Formal education will make you a living. Self-education will make you a fortune.—Jim Rohn*

- ❖ *Ask a question and you're a fool for three minutes; do not ask a question and you're a fool for the rest of your life.*
  —Chinese Proverb

- ❖ *The man who is too old to learn was probably always too old to learn.—Henry S. Haskins*

- ❖ *The purpose of learning is growth, and our minds, unlike our bodies, can continue growing as we continue to live.*
  —Mortimer Adler

- ❖ *Formal education will make you a living. Self-education will make you a fortune.—Jim Rohn*

- ❖ *Ask a question and you're a fool for three minutes; do not ask a question and you're a fool for the rest of your life.*
  —Chinese Proverb

- ❖ *The man who is too old to learn was probably always too old to learn.—Henry S. Haskins*

- ❖ *The purpose of learning is growth, and our minds, unlike our bodies, can continue growing as we continue to live.*
  —Mortimer Adler

RECOMMENDED ACTION STEPS

1) Keep a note of how any goals and objectives you have are being hindered (or are likely to be hindered) due to lack of relevant information or know-how.

2) Make a point of learn what you need to learn in order to accomplish your objectives successfully. Add these knowledge and skill requirements to your learning goals and your to-do list.

3) Resolve to do (1) and (2) above, rather than rely on guesswork, especially where outcomes are important or critical.

PART THREE

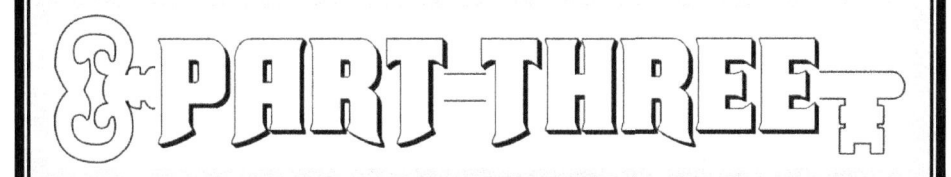

WEALTH: WAYS TO GET IT, KEEP IT AND INCREASE IT

If wealth is part of your ambition, then there is certainly scope for great wealth to be built using the techniques herein! This Part of the book may not be the most important one for you, if you are already in possession of a high level of financial security and competence, or if you are simply not concerned about material gain and material affluence. However this part is still packed with potent insights from which you may someday wish to profit, or intimate to a son, daughter or a grandchild. It's worth exploring, if only to make sure you aren't missing anything that you might wish to implement, to your tremendous advantage!

❖ *If we command our wealth, we shall be rich and free. If our wealth commands us, we are poor indeed. —Edmund Burke*

16
REFLECTIONS ON WEALTH
AND THE VALUE OF MONEY

❖ *Happiness is not in the mere possession of money; it lies in the joy of achievement, in the thrill of creative effort.*
—*Franklin D. Roosevelt*

Rather than immediately go all-out on the acquisition of unlimited wealth at all costs, it makes sense to look carefully at the subject of wealth, to determine what it means for us and how much we are really willing to pay for it.

The foremost secret of building wealth is to make more than your living expenses, and invest the difference wisely. Please read that again, and remember it well.

With that established, let us now consider the subject of wealth itself, so that you will hopefully be better equipped to set meaningful goals that promote true self-fulfillment. It helps us to develop worthwhile goals if we understand the nature of wealth, and the real value of money.

Many assume that wealth always equals self-fulfillment. This is not always true, because self-fulfillment is about inner peace and ultimate happiness, and money can't always buy this. Some things are more valuable than money, and many people overlook this. To achieve true self-fulfillment, we cannot afford such oversights.

Real wealth

Most people equate wealth to the amount of money they own. But this is short-sighted. If you hunger for financial wealth, try looking one stage further—ask yourself why you want the money. What real benefits will it bring? Most people will agree that when they think about it, it's not the money that they ultimately want, but the happiness, satisfaction, security and peace of mind they believe it will bring. Financial wealth doesn't automatically deliver all these things.

What is money, really?

If the real rewards in life are happiness, satisfaction, joy, etc., then the relatively poor person can be more successful than the billionaire. It's not the amount of money that counts, but how much you appreciate what you have and how well you use it. It's not uncommon to find rich people whose timetables are so full that they rarely take holidays, or enjoy themselves in other ways. Often we see relatively poor people who somehow manage to spend much more time having fun and enjoying life—accumulating a rich storehouse of good memories: something that can never be taken away from them.

A beggar can be more successful than a millionaire. Suppose the millionaire is never satisfied—always craving more of everything, without ever truly enjoying what he has. Suppose he feels he has no real friends; that all the people in his life are primarily only interested in sharing his wealth, or enjoying the prestige of being acquainted with him. Suppose he loses sleep at night, worried about whether his extensive assets will be decimated by the latest economic crisis. Suppose the millionaire has chronic depression.

Suppose, on the other hand, that the poor man has friends who he loves and trusts implicitly and has been happy all his life. Who is the wealthier in real terms? The millionaire has money, but that can easily be lost. Our beggar, on the other hand, has a rich treasure trove of wonderful memories—something that money cannot buy and no-one can take away. This is not to say that you have to be poor in order to be happy; simply that money is not the measure of true wealth and success.

Most people realize this—even if deeply within their subconscious mind. This is precisely why building financial wealth is so hard for most people. It's because they don't really have their heart and soul in it. Their wiser, subconscious mind is always working against them, trying to deter them from continuing with such distorted values. The sages and prophets of old often described money as a false god; the love of money is described as a root of evil. These are wise words; money does indeed have a misleading allure that all too often seduces people into making shameful sacrifices to acquire it. Money is only a worthwhile objective if it is part of a plan to achieve something of real value: something that falls into line with your deepest convictions, your basic philosophy and your ultimate code of living—something that your heart and soul are truly behind.

❖ *That man is the richest whose pleasures are the cheapest.*
   —Henry David Thoreau

How can we achieve real wealth?

We've established then, that money alone cannot buy lasting happiness. We've established also that monitory wealth is always relative; it's not a fixed reality that we can achieve, resulting in lasting satisfaction. Much psychological research has been done to find out what *really* satisfies people; the things people ultimately want money for; the real basic human drives. The psychologist Abraham Maslow was a great contributor to this field. He managed to identify five basic drives that all people tend to have. Since his research, a further drive has been identified: the need for intellectual stimulation, making six in all.

The pyramid of basic human drives

```
              /\
             /  \
            / The need \
           / for self-realization \
          /──────────────\
         /   The need     \
        /  for recognition  \
       /──────────────────\
      /    The need for     \
     /   love and belonging   \
    /──────────────────────\
   /   The intellectual needs   \
  /──────────────────────────\
 /     The need for security     \
/──────────────────────────────\
/   The basic physiological needs  \
────────────────────────────────────
```

MASLOW'S PYRAMID OF BASIC HUMAN DRIVES

First of all, at the bottom of the pyramid, every individual is driven to satisfy his basic bodily needs. That is, the need for physical survival—the need for food, water, air to breathe, warmth, etc.

Only after those needs are satisfied, will his desire be directed to the need for security: the assurance that he isn't going to die at any moment; the need for a safe home to go to; the need to know he is safe from upheavals, physical assault, disease, etc.

After that drive is satisfied, intellectual needs take precedence: the need to understand, the need to find out, the need for new experiences. After that, he will start to desire companionship, love and belonging.

After that, he will yearn for recognition, or esteem—a feeling of pride and self-value—the needs of the ego.

Even when that need is satisfied, a person will still feel another drive—the need for self-realization. This is the need to live at one's full potential. It's the drive that makes people want to improve their lives, and to do their best.

These then, are the real drives: the ones people seek to satisfy through the ownership of money. Certainly, money has a convenient purpose, but we must get its value into perspective. There may often be a much more immediate and effective way to satisfy your basic drives than by slowly and painfully striving to acquire the money that we think will satisfy our needs. Often, money will come as a natural result of finding ways to satisfy the highest drive—that of self-realization. The great artists and scientists rarely do their work motivated by money. They do it primarily to satisfy the need for self-realization.

Most people crave money because they believe it will bring a feeling of security and prestige. They are usually disappointed, finding that they feel less secure with the money than they did without it. They find also that the prestige is elusive; they soon discover that there are even wealthier 'Jones's' to keep up with; wealth is always relative.

Money is simply a conversion medium we use to change one form of value into another. The money in itself has no intrinsic value (it won't help you if you are dying of an incurable disease, or are stranded on a desert island).

Money usually has a role to play in satisfying the first drive, and to some degree the second and even the third, but it is only needed in moderate amounts. After those three drives are satisfied, money seems to have less significance. Love and belonging cannot be bought with money; they are the rewards of inner qualities. Gone are the days when having money meant recognition and esteem. People nowadays are much more likely to value a person for his inner qualities. After all, some of the greatest contributors to our culture have been poor.

So money in itself is not one of the prime motivators, and the further up the pyramid we go, the less important it becomes. Self-realization is the ultimate goal. Money has a lot of potential, but only if we have a worthy, predetermined use for it.

Wealth redefined

Real wealth then, is not the amount of money you have, but how well you are able to use it, and the degree to which you can satisfy your basic drives. In other words, how much happiness you have.

Is money the ultimate liquid asset? No, our ultimate asset is our capacity to render useful service; our ability to improve the quality of other people's lives. In other words, our skills and talents, provided they are in demand. There's little value in offering service X, if a million and one other practitioners are offering the same service, unless you can find some way of offering better value than theirs.

We only live once (or so we are told). Who then is the wiser (and wealthier, in real terms): (1) the person who spends his life in toil and strife, trying to accumulate money, never satisfying his higher drives, and who has few good memories to look back on as he gets old, or (2) the person who manages himself so effectively that he satisfies all his drives, enjoying life ever more each day, thus building a wealth of good memories?

Seven cures for a lean purse

The following 'Seven Cures For a Lean Purse' are from the best-selling classic on happiness and prosperity, *The Richest Man in Babylon,* by George S. Clayton. In 1926, he wrote: "Lo, money is plentiful for those who understand the simple rules of its acquisition"...

1st Cure: Start thy purse to fattening

2nd Cure: Control thy expenditure

3rd Cure: Make thy gold multiply

4th Cure: Guard thy treasures from loss

5th Cure: Make the dwelling a profitable investment

6th Cure: Insure a future Income

7th Cure: Increase thy ability to earn

- *A man is rich in proportion to the things he can afford to let alone.—Henry David Thoreau*

- *Money never made a man happy yet, nor will it. There is nothing in its nature to produce happiness. The more a man has, the more he wants. Instead of filling a vacuum, it makes one.—Benjamin Franklin*

- *I've learned that making a 'living' is not the same thing as 'making a life'. —Maya Angelou*

- *Make money your god and he will plague you like the devil. —Henry Fielding*

- *Riches begin in the form of thought.* —Napoleon Hill
- *Fortunes gravitate to men whose minds have been prepared to attract them just as surely as water gravitates to the ocean.* —Napoleon Hill

RECOMMENDED ACTION STEP

Review your goals and ask yourself if they are based on a truly wise and intelligent value system. Do your main life goals promote your ultimate happiness and fulfillment? If not, then redefine your goals accordingly.

❖ *If money is your hope for independence you will never have it. The only real security that a man will have in this world is a reserve of knowledge, experience, and ability.*
—Henry Ford

17
CAREER DEVELOPMENT
TO HASTEN FINANCIAL SECURITY

❖ *It's not what you achieve, it's what you overcome. That's what defines your career.* —Carlton Fisk

The care you take in planning the steps you take on the pathway of your career has an inestimable payoff in terms of return on time and effort invested. This chapter looks at ways to make the best career decisions. It shares the key tactics and strategies you can adopt for maximal progress throughout your career. It is never too late to adopt these pivotal strategies.

In this chapter, we will uncover some special power-strategies that can make a massive difference to your career success. These simple strategies make people into millionaires, while those who overlook or ignore them can become tragic failures. We only get one life, and these strategies can maximize your chances of making the most of it. They can be applied at any stage of your career, but the sooner you adopt them, the better your prospects will be.

In today's world it is harder than ever to become financially successful – especially if you are not fortunate enough to have been born into wealth—and even this is no guarantee of success. Today, competition in the commercial world is tougher than ever.

But we can still succeed, armed with the right strategies. We have already covered many powerful strategies and approaches throughout this book, but in this chapter we'll cover some that specifically focus on one's career. Countless people in this country who are now struggling to get by, could have become millionaires before reaching 40, had they followed the strategies that follow.

Employment vs. self-employment

Firstly, it's important to know that most of the fortunes that have been built by self-made men and women who started out with very little, have been accumulated through some form of enterprise rather than through regular employment. That's partly because when employed by someone else, a large portion of the returns on your productivity is retained by your employer, and you are primarily working to make your employer rich.

It is also important to note, however, that a large percentage of entrepreneurs fail on their first attempt at business. Invariably this is because of some oversight or careless planning that could have been avoided. If you venture into entrepreneurship, make every possible effort not to be one of these first-time failures!

Of course, you may not be in a position to embark on a business venture at the present time. This may be because you have convinced yourself that you are not suited to it – or it could simply be that you haven't come up with a viable idea or business plan yet. Self-employment is not for everyone.

In any case, you still have 'Plan B' open to you: the more common route of regular employment. Many people reading this will now be thinking, "Yes, but how can I ever build up wealth with the few skills I have?"

The answer is: "You'd be surprised!" I could give you a list of multimillionaires who built up their wealth from almost nothing, starting with only menial skills, who succeeded through dogged persistence and careful planning. Bill Gates, one of the richest people on the planet, is a case in point.

Most people who started out with almost nothing yet built fabulous wealth over time, are likely to have implemented one or more of the all-important wealth strategies we are about to uncover.

Think of jobs as stepping stones

The first of these strategies is fairly easy to implement and yet most people just don't bother – even though they know it makes sense! We've just mentioned how working for an employer primarily serves to help your employer become more wealthy and successful, while your own best interests are secondary at best, from his point of view. So the obvious thing to do is to 'use' your employer in much the same way he, she, or it, is using you! What do I mean exactly? I mean that you can stay in the employment for the time being while you are gaining new skills and building some sort of additional personal value that can go onto your next CV.

So, unless you work for a company or organization that is your ultimate dream, to which you are dedicated for life, think of your job as a stepping stone on your path to self-betterment.

Always negotiate your salary!

It is amazing how many employees just accept whatever salary they are offered, without any attempt to negotiate. When you go for a job interview, your potential employer is naturally going to offer you as little as possible. In most cases, he could afford to pay more, and will do, if you ask for more, pointing out that you think you could earn more elsewhere. If you get a curt, inflexible reply, well, at least you tried! You may even earn some respect for making that effort. However, always negotiate with finesse, tact and diplomacy to avoid causing irritation and to maximize your chances of success.

Once you have settled in to the new job, your skills within the company will naturally develop, and this makes you more valuable to your employer. So naturally, it makes sense to make an effort to negotiate a higher salary as soon as this situation arrives.

Don't stay too long!

As soon as you find that you are learning little new, and your salary seems to have become disinclined to increase, it's very likely a good time to move on - onto the next step up your career ladder. You can do this by applying for other jobs while you are still in the present job. Some people will be thinking "But I just don't have any energy to spare after my employer has been slave-driving me all week!" Well, I'm not suggesting you devote a great deal of time to looking for that better job. You only need to get into the routine of devoting enough time to apply for one or two jobs every week. This can take up as little as an hour a week. Once you have your CV written up, most of the work is already done.

Unless your skills are in exceptionally high demand, be prepared to face a lot of disappointments in the form of job-refusals. This is absolutely normal. Think of it as a numbers game. If you keep applying for a new job, eventually you will get lucky – but ONLY if you keep trying! Most people give up almost immediately and resign themselves to continuing in their current employment with no real plan to climb out of the rut. But you know better, don't you? And when you do get offered that next step up the employment ladder, into a better paid job that teaches you new skills that you can add to your CV, you will feel ecstatic, because you have proven yourself to be one of a very special breed: the upwardly mobile! That is a very important status to have – and it can soon be achieved, even if you are starting off at the bottom of your career ladder, flipping burgers or washing cars.

Before you make that next step into the new job, you can, if you wish, use the new job offer as a bargaining point to push for a better salary from your old employer! Employers are notorious for taking their employees for granted. If they suddenly realize they are in danger of losing you, your real value will suddenly become apparent. If you succeed in obtaining an offer of a pay rise from your old employer, you can then reconsider whether you want to move on.

Education and training

The next strategy concerns education. Many people make the mistake of thinking that if they get a degree, they will be made for life. The sad truth however, is that most people who obtain a degree don't even manage to land a job that makes use of it! That's partly because most employers today are wise enough to realize that certain qualities of character, together with relevant work experience, take precedence over any scholarly certificate the applicant may have.

Embarking on a course of further education can be a massive investment of time and expense, and in most cases, it doesn't guarantee you a job at the end of it.

There is nothing intrinsically wrong with developing your knowledge and expertise through the education, of course. And it is mandatory to have a degree in order to gain access to some professions, but it's important to get formal education into perspective, because of the various potential pitfalls.

Some drawbacks of formal education

It is important to be aware of the potential pitfalls before committing to a long and expensive course of further education. Here are a few of them:

Many of the tutors teaching degree courses have no professional experience in the subject they are teaching! I recall when I did a course in business studies, I had several questions that I needed answering. When I approached the tutor, he had to admit he couldn't answer my questions because he had never been in business! He had only ever been a teacher of business! Academic knowledge is a poor substitute for real-world experience.

Can you really predict your future ambitions?

A degree takes years to attain. Unless you are absolutely certain that you will still be interested in your career of choice when you finish your further education, you could end up in a career you hate.

Inefficient learning

College and university learning can be terribly inefficient. You will probably have to endure the soul-destroying drudgery of learning reams of outdated or irrelevant material that you may never need to know in the real commercial world. In terms of time and cost, it is often much more expedient to teach yourself—as long as a printed certificate is not an absolute prerequisite to your chosen career path. One year of work experience in a carefully-chosen industry could do more for your employability than a year in university.

❖ *Formal education will make you a living; self-education will make you fortune.*---Jim Rohn

The cost

Then there is the cost. Many people borrow money to finance their education. Starting your career saddled with debt is definitely not ideal, so think carefully if the course you are considering doesn't even guarantee you a job at its completion.

Times change

A degree course can take years to complete. Meanwhile the world is moving ahead, ever changing, and the rate of change is now faster than it has ever been since the Industrial Revolution. Furthermore the direction of the changes are not easy to predict. How can you be sure that the degree you aspire to will still be such a useful asset in four years' time? Degrees tend to be in very narrow areas of expertise, giving you access to a very narrow industrial sector. Real-world work experience, on the other hand, is more likely to give you a number of useful skills that will serve you well in a broader range of careers or professions.

Avoiding debt - unless it makes you wealthier

The third important strategy concerns debt. Debt has become so commonplace in today's world, that it's easy to succumb to the notion that debt is fine, dandy and normal. In truth, debt can be like a disease. If not controlled or properly understood, it can increasingly sap your life blood like some parasite that is very difficult to eradicate. So the third key strategy to wealth building is to avoid debt from the outset (if humanly possible)—or, if you already have debt, to pay it off as soon as humanly possible. Otherwise, making progress towards financial freedom will be like trying to get ahead with a bloated vampire clinging to your neck by its fangs—a vampire that can't be dispatched with a simple wooden stake. If you have several loans, and you are able to spare some of your income for paying them off, focus on paying off the one with the highest rate of interest first!

Debt is such a burden and so potentially hazardous, that the only time you'd be wise to touch it with a barge pole is when you can use it to genuinely make you richer. One example might be to take out a mortgage for a home if you know you can cope with the repayments. It may well make sense to do that if making the repayments will cost less than it would to rent a home and also if property values are rising to the extent that you are likely to make a profit even after the total of your interest repayments has been factored in.

Buying and selling for profit

Buying and selling, as a part time venture, has the advantage of requiring no academic or industrial qualifications. Anyone with some spare cash can do it. It's a good idea to look for some type of commodity that has not yet been fully exploited but which has the potential to grow in popularity in the future. The earlier you can jump on the bandwagon, the easier it is to be the market leader in that field. However, bear in mind that NOTHING is absolutely certain in this world (except death and taxes, as the tongue-in-cheek saying goes).

If you can find something you can buy and then quickly resell at 100% profit, that's great. If you find you are successful, you will probably want to keep repeating the process. Not only will your working fund increase but so will your expertise. Make sure you pick some product that you can sell quickly, because accumulating unsold stock is to be avoided at all costs. That's why many dealers occasionally sell off stock at zero profit. Better to sell at zero profit than not sell at all! At least you end up with some cash to make REAL profits with. With the exception of some collectables and antiques, most things start depreciating in value the moment they leave the factory, so that's another reason not to get lumbered with stock any longer than is necessary.

A spare-time venture

Be very careful, because it is very easy to be duped into buying something that looks like an incredible bargain, thinking you can *definitely* sell it quickly and double your money, when in fact doing so may be difficult or even impossible. So aim to know the field before you dip your toe into something which could be as hazardous as nitric acid!

Selling your skills as a sideline

Buying and selling things as a sideline is not for everyone. Some people fare better selling their skills as a sideline venture. The great advantage of this is that no merchandise is involved, so the risk of loss, damage and depreciation is removed. Furthermore your savings can probably remain untouched and therefore safe.

Whichever option you choose (selling your skills or selling some commodity), you can start small and expand as time passes and your skills, funds and knowledge grow.

Keep living costs to a bare minimum

Saving money regularly is easier to accomplish if you keep your living costs to a bare minimum. That's another thing that too many people fail to do. Many people who are stuck in the rut of a boring job use retail therapy as a form of drug, to dull the distress of having to endure a job that isn't helping them fulfill their dreams and ambitions. That's almost as bad as turning to drink or drugs! Retail therapy is most easily avoided when one is totally absorbed in bettering oneself in some way.

Go where the money is!

Here is another key strategy. This is so obvious that it should go without saying, yet most people fail to implement it: **Go where the money is!!** It is pointless having abilities, if few people within reach have any money to pay for your skills. Again, we are talking about a numbers game. If you go where the money is, the law of averages ensures that you will have a much easier time finding clients and customers eager to cross your palm with silver.

At this point, many people will be thinking: "But what about the Internet? That puts the moneyed people of the whole world at my fingertips, doesn't it? So why should I bother to move?" Well, the very considerable downside of the Internet, is that those big spenders are also at the fingertips of all of your competitors, *worldwide!* And the chances are, there will be people out there (perhaps in some poorer country) that will be willing to work a lot harder than you are for the same money, or less!

So it is of great advantage to become part of a moneyed community or locality, where you can become known – where people can receive recommendations about you from their friends and colleagues, and where they can get to meet you in the flesh. Remember: not everyone looks to the Internet for everything they need.

- *Choose a job you love, and you will never have to work a day in your life. —Confucius*
- *It's not what you achieve, it's what you overcome. That's what defines your career. —Carlton Fisk*
- *No one can discover you until you do. Exploit your talents, skills and strengths and make the world sit up and take notice. —Rob Liano*
- *Some people make enough, some people don't, and it has nothing to do with their paycheck. —Janene Murphy*
- *Work to become, not to acquire. —Elbert Hubbard*
- *If you don't wake up in the morning excited to pick up where you left your work yesterday, you haven't found your calling yet. —Mike Wallace*

RECOMMENDED ACTION STEPS

1) Re-read this chapter and make one or more new goals based on the insights gained from this chapter.
2) Resolve to implement the strategies we have covered here.

18
BUILDING WEALTH
WITH EXPONENTIAL GROWTH

❖ *Rich old people are more attractive than poor old people, so by all means, try to get rich before age sets in. Otherwise, you'll just be playing catch-up for the rest of your life and that will just wear you out, let me tell you.*
—Jill Conner Browne

Apart from the obvious approach of maximizing our income, there are other, perhaps even more important strategies we can employ to maximize the growth of our equity in order to achieve financial freedom and independence.

Perhaps the most important first step to building wealth, is to properly understand debt, its dangers and ramifications. In most cases, the most important step in building increasing wealth is to clear any debt you may have – especially if the cost of that debt is more than the amount it is increasing your equity. (Equity is the sum of your wealth after the sum of your debt has been subtracted.)

The second most basic and important axiom of wealth building is to earn more than you spend, and to invest the difference wisely.

It is also financially responsible to maintain some savings and if you are able, to keep adding to that fund continuously. It is wise to regard that fund as precious and resolve to use it only in ways that will make you richer. Any fool can spend money, but it takes real skill to make it. Remember that money of itself is only a means to an end. There is little satisfaction in striving for it for its own sake, so it is important to have a long-term vision of where you want to go, and to have a strategy for getting there.

It is a good strategy to set aside at least one tenth of your income regularly in a bank account with the best rate of interest available. Most people can cope with saving just ten per cent. You may find you can easily cover that much by spending more carefully and cutting back on self-defeating luxuries that do nothing to promote your ultimate goals.

Saving regularly - and take advantage of compound interest

After you have paid off any debt you are burdened with, the next step is to start saving money regularly—and I mean very regularly, and take full advantage of compound interest. I recommend that you leave this growing fund untouched, with only two possible exceptions: (1) an absolute emergency, and (2) if you find some safe way of multiplying some of your fund through buying and selling something for a quick and certain profit. The following chart illustrates the results of saving regularly, both with and without compound interest. Compound interest differs from simple interest in that interest is added, calculated on your savings, plus the interest that has already been added. That is where it differs from simple interest.

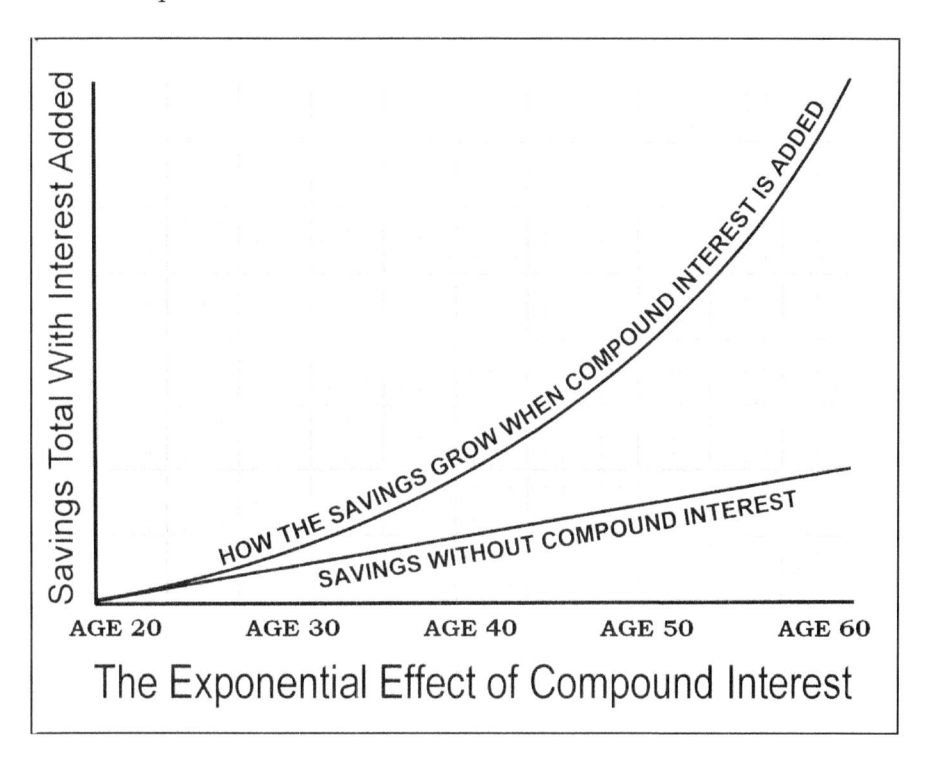

The Exponential Effect of Compound Interest

Look for ways to multiply the money even faster

While you are saving this tenth of all you earn, look for ways you can put your savings to work even more profitably. If you see something that you can buy for $X, knowing you can definitely sell it straight away to Mr Jones for $X times two, go for it! If possible, get Jones' agreement to buy before you commit your money to the purchase. After the sale, take your doubled money and repeat the exercise, armed with the experience you've gained. Building wealth can be that simple!

If you do find a way of doubling your money with a single sale and with no overheads to pay, there is much to be excited about. To illustrate this: if you start out with an investment of just one dollar and make a 200% return (i.e. 100% profit) which happens frequently enough, you end up with $2. Repeat the exercise, investing your $2 and making $4. You need only repeat this pattern 21 times, and your 21st sale will net you OVER TWO MILLION DOLLARS! If you don't believe it, check the figures with a calculator; the result of each successive sale is shown in the table that follows.

Certainly, it is easier said than done to double your money on every sale, but if you make it your goal, even if you don't achieve that ideal, you'll be doing okay! As you are doing this with your 10%-of-income set-aside fund, rather than with your 'bread and butter' living expense money, you are not forced to make a sale every day. You can wait until you find an investment that will net you 100% profit if you wish. Then you will only have to make 21 such operations in order to make the kind of money shown in the following table.

With an initial investment of only $1,
making a 200% return on every sale
and reinvesting 100% of the proceeds of each sale:

Income, sale #1:	$2.00
Income, sale #2:	$4.00
Income, sale #3:	$8.00
Income, sale #4:	$16.00
Income, sale #5:	$32.00
Income, sale #6:	$64.00
Income, sale #7:	$128.00
Income, sale #8:	$256.00
Income, sale #9:	$512.00
Income, sale #10:	$1,024.00
Income, sale #11:	$2,048.00
Income, sale #12:	$4,096.00
Income, sale #13:	$8,192.00
Income, sale #14:	$16,384.00
Income, sale #15:	$32,768.00
Income, sale #16:	$65,536.00
Income, sale #17:	$131,072.00
Income, sale #18:	$262,144.00
Income, sale #19:	$524,288.00
Income, sale #20:	$1,048,576.00
Income, sale #21:	$2,097,152.00

Exponential growth

In the table above, your money is multiplying at a rapid but also exponential rate. That is to say that the curve on a chart of your returns gets steeper and steeper as time passes! While making 100% profit on every sale is not always easy to achieve, the good news is that no matter what percentage profit you make each time, provided it is more than zero, after subtracting any overheads (expenses incurred in the process of completing the operation), exponential growth of your fund can still be achieved. However, the more profit you make on each sale, the more rapidly the growth of your fund will accelerate.

You might argue that no-one can make such exciting increases in wealth, because they have to draw off something for living expenses. Not in this case! Remember, I suggested that you put aside 10% of your income solely for putting into some form of growth enterprise such as buying and selling. You don't use any of your profits for living expenses; you plough it all straight back into your next purchase.

Even if you play ultra-safe and merely leave your money in a savings account that pays compound interest, it will still grow exponentially as long as you leave it alone. In fact, if you put a lump sum into an account that pays 7% per annum, your money will approximately double every ten years. That is the wonder of compound interest.

Consider your long-term future

Consider carefully your future needs. None of us wants to end up lonely and poor. If you don't already have the enterprise mentality, develop one. Making money invariably takes a lot of time and long hours of hard work, so it makes perfect sense to get into a line of work or business that gives you satisfaction for its own sake. The money will follow you. At the end of the day, it is more important to enjoy your time and use it wisely in ways that give you self-respect. You can always replace lost money but you can never replace lost time. All the money in the world will not give you satisfaction towards the end of your life when time is running out and you look back on your life in self-judgment.

❖ *If a man goes into business with only the idea of making money, chances are he won't. —Joyce Clyde Hall*

❖ *The habit of saving is itself an education; it fosters every virtue, teaches self-denial, cultivates the sense of order, trains to forethought, and so broadens the mind.*
   —T.T. Munger

❖ *Let him who would enjoy a good future waste none of his present. —Roger Babson*

RECOMMENDED ACTION STEPS

1) Calculate carefully what your week to week living expenses amount to.

2) If your living expenses amount to more than your income, look for ways to cut them back until they are less than your living expenses.

3) Use the difference to pay off any debt you have.

4) When you are debt-free, set the excess income aside regularly. Aim to set aside at least 10% of your income for your future.

5) Take full advantage of the magic of exponential growth from compound interest or from repeatedly buying and selling something profitably.

19
DEBT: A TWO-EDGED SWORD
NOT TO BE PLAYED WITH

❖ *Rather go to bed supperless, than rise in debt.*
  —Benjamin Franklin

Understanding credit (a flattering word that means debt), is essential for financial success. Then you can gain advantage from it in certain circumstances, and avoid becoming a slave to it. This chapter explores the basics.

Credit is having the use of assets for which it is agreed that payment may be deferred. In other words, it's having the use of things you don't have to pay for immediately. These may be:

- **Money**—for example when you borrow money from a bank, by taking an overdraft or by using a credit card. (Both are simply two forms of bank loan.)
- **Goods or services**—when someone sells you something and agrees that you can pay later. (Between businesses, the majority of dealings are of this type.)

Most loans incur interest—a predetermined price you pay for the privileges of using someone else's money. This can be anything from 0% to over 1,000% per annum. Loan sharks and payday loan specialists usually charge high rates of interest, while regular banks often charge very low rates of interest. Some retailers (car dealers in particular) will often entice people to buy by offering 0% interest rates. This way, you can pay monthly rather than all at once, but pay no extra for that privilege.

A useful but dangerous tool

To a business, whether it is a multinational corporation or a self-employed individual, credit is an extremely valuable facility. This is because businesses can make money out of money. The more it has available, the more it can make, and the less hard it has to work for it.

Credit is a valuable aid if used with careful discretion. That is to say, with full awareness of the risks and dangers of borrowing money. Let's consider two imaginary aspirants:

Bob Struggler and Jim Skimmer. Both were carpenters working at a factory. The factory has just made them redundant. Bob and Jim both have ideas about going self-employed.

Bob Struggler's tale

Bob doesn't have a bank account, and doesn't know anyone who is able or willing to lend him money. Because he cannot get credit from anywhere he is at a big disadvantage as far as making money is concerned. He can still make money, but he only has his existing assets to help him. That is, his skills, his tools, his good health, his contacts and his home workshop, for example. He scratches together enough money to buy some timber with which to make a cabinet that he can then sell. He works away at the cabinet, with aching belly because he has nothing to eat, and two weeks later, it's finished and ready to sell.

Jim Skimmer's tale

Jim, on the other hand, has a bank account. Because he has used his money responsibly, the manager has allowed him an overdraft facility. He can now draw out $200 more than he actually owns. The bank trusts him to pay it back. Jim thinks about ways of making money. Having studied this book, he thoroughly takes stock of his assets. His attention settles upon that $200 overdraft facility. Somewhat excited, he realizes that he doesn't have to spend two weeks making a cabinet before he can eat. He knows a man who's looking for a handsome cabinet for his collection of glassware, and he knows exactly what kind of cabinet is required. He forms a plan. He draws out the $200 and buys a second-hand cabinet from Bert's used furniture store for $80. He then takes it to Ken the French polisher (who was also made redundant by the factory), and pays him $100 to restore it to pristine condition. The next day, he sells it to the glass-collecting cabinet-seeker for $400. He's made $200 profit, and he only worked for three hours to achieve it. If he does the same thing every day for the next week, he makes $1,400 profit without even working up a sweat. He then pays the original $200 back to the bank. While he's at the bank, he tells the bank manager what he did. He explains that if only he had been able to borrow $600 instead of $200, he could have made much more money. He could have bought genuine antique cabinets, and sold them for a fortune after having had them restored. The manager agrees to increase the overdraft facility. Jim goes on to make much more money. Bob, on the other hand, has toiled away in his home workshop for two weeks, and finally sells his cabinet for $400. From this he must subtract the money he paid for timber, new saw blades, and many other odds and ends. He ends up with just under $200 profit in the same amount of time. The purpose of this story is to illustrate that credit can be effectively used to make money (not to advocate the benefits of cabinet-making).

It sometimes makes sense to work with borrowed money, when a quick profit can be made and the loan can be paid back quickly. If it cannot be repaid quickly, the interest still has to be paid. If the borrower doesn't keep up to date with the interest repayments, the interest can mount up, placing one increasingly deeper in debt until such time as the loan is repaid. Unless a fixed rate of interest has been agreed, there is also a danger that interest rates may rise, so always bear this in mind when considering the pros and cons of taking out a loan.

Ted Blewitt's tale

Now let's look at a third carpenter from the factory: Ted Blewitt. Ted also has a bank account with a $200 overdraft facility. He follows the same plan as Jim—with one exception: he didn't take the trouble to find out exactly what kind of cabinet the glass-collector wanted. He goes ahead and buys an old cabinet. He has it restored to its former glory and offers it to the glass collector.

Unfortunately it is not to the glass-collector's taste and he flatly refuses it. Although Ted thought it was a fine piece of furniture, it was a style of cabinet that no one wants these days. He is now in a difficult predicament. He has to find the money to put the cabinet into storage, and to advertize it in the local paper, in the hopes that someone somewhere will want such a piece. He also has to pay charges to the bank for the $200 loan which he is currently unable to pay back.

With all this to worry about, he also has to find money enough to eat, so he resorts to Bob Struggler's plan, and starts making his own furniture. He has to work much harder than Bob though, because he has these extra liabilities. The extra liabilities make him worry, so he can't work so efficiently. On top of all this, they prevent him from affording the proper tools for the job. He ends up having a much harder time than Bob, and probably won't realize as much profit. He falls out of favor with the bank manager because he can't repay his loan, and loses his right to borrow in the future.

When to borrow

Here is the golden rule when you are considering using credit: Ask yourself, "Will this enable me to make or save more money than the cost of the loan?"

Most people only have a limited amount of credit available. Therefore that credit should be treated as a precious asset and used only with the most careful consideration. Don't waste it like the fellow who stretches himself to the limit to buy a new car on credit, just to upgrade his image in the hope of suddenly becoming a social success. He finds himself working like a slave to keep up the payments. Was a new car really necessary? It's a high price to pay for a better image. It's unlikely that it will bring sufficient benefits to justify the extra work and the loss of freedom that goes with it.

The price of credit can be the loss of your freedom. Many first-time buyers come up against this realization when they finally move into their new house, and come face to face with the loss of the freedom they have just signed away. The value of freedom should never be forgotten. So many people in the world are unhappy for most of their lives because they have given up too much freedom. Desire is what leads you to lose your freedom—desire for possessions, whether it be a house or a spouse. So here's a golden rule of success: If you desire something enough to sacrifice your freedom for it, make sure it is something that brings you more freedom, overall, when all is said and done.

Handle with caution if interest will be charged

Don't be one of the millions of unsuccessful people who are slaves to material possessions that they never really needed anyway. The problem is that people are usually able to get more credit than is good for them.

Example: Bank A decides that Mrs Wantit is to be allowed a $1,000 limit on her credit card. The problems start when about six other establishments also give her $1,000 credit: stores, mail-order outlets, second bank account and so on. Gradually, Mrs Wantit finds herself with a monthly liability of about $500 per month, plus an insatiable appetite for luxury goods.

Many stores are eager to get people to buy their goods on credit using their own finance companies. They know that most people don't have the resources to lay out cash for expensive items. If they didn't offer credit, they wouldn't be able to sell enough goods to stay in business.

So borrow money only if it enables you to make money. Never buy anything on credit purely on impulse. Always think very carefully about what the loan is going to cost you. Take into account things like:

- The total interest you'll pay (total of all the monthly interest payments).
- The consequential loss of credit availability (everyone has a credit limit).
- The risk. What will happen if you lose your job and are unable to pay.
- The inconvenience of having to make regular payments.
- The loss of freedom.

If you are in business, you need to be even more mathematical about it. How much profit will the loan enable you to make? What is the interest on the loan? How many times can you use that money to multiply itself while you have it on loan?

Defer payment if possible

If you have the option of not having to pay for something immediately, it makes sense to take advantage of this in most situations. Most household utility payments, for example, can be spread out over a long period or deferred for thirty days without any interest charges. Until the agreed latest payment date, you have the use of the money—interest free. Most inter-business dealings operate under thirty-day payment terms, and this thirty-day leeway is usually exploited to the full. However there are situations, where a business may opt to pay its bills almost immediately—for example, if it wishes to earn itself a special favored status, with future deals in mind.

Don't play with fire!

Would you let a toddler play with a box of matches? I wouldn't, but many banks do (in effect)! They lend money to folks who don't have even a basic understanding of the workings of debt and compound interest. Hopefully this chapter offers some insight into the way credit works. However, if there is anything about it that you don't understand, please find someone who can explain it to you properly so that you understand it. The ramifications of not doing so are serious. If you borrow money or buy on credit without understanding the way interest can build up, you are truly 'playing with fire'. Unfortunately, too many people who don't understand the mechanics of debt are falling prey to ruthless loan sharks who charge massive rates of interest, and they quickly become slaves living in fear and dread.

❖ *Home life ceases to be free and beautiful as soon as it is founded on borrowing and debt. —Henrik Ibsen*

❖ *Debt, (n): an ingenious substitute for the chain and whip of the slave driver. —Ambrose Bierce*

RECOMMENDED ACTION STEPS

(for those who have debts, i.e. loans outstanding)

1) Make it one of your most important priorities to get rid of your debts as soon as possible by whatever means.

2) Make a list of any assets you could sell off to pay down your debts.

3) List all the ways you could reduce your monthly expenditure and divert the saving into paying down your debts.

4) If you have more than one loan, focus on paying off the one with the highest interest rate first.

5) Find out if you can transfer one or more of your debts to a different lender who charges a lower interest rate.

6) Many credit card providers offer 0% interest for several months initially. See if you can take advantage of this, but stay vigilant regarding the expiry of the 0% period, because when it expires, the interest may rise to a punitive level. Make sure you know what that level is!

7) Keep accurate records of the status of your debts, ideally using a computer spreadsheet. Carefully review it once a month or more.

20
SUCCESSFUL NEGOTIATING
A PIVOTAL SUCCESS SKILL

❖ *Let us never negotiate out of fear. But let us never fear to negotiate.* —John F. Kennedy

The art of negotiating is one of the most important skills you can acquire, as a success seeker. This skill can make all the difference in many areas in life. Much more is negotiable than the average person realizes. In this chapter we reveal some universal strategies and skills to focus on.

The meek may inherit the earth, but in the meantime, they would do well to develop their negotiating skills! Are you one of the meek, when it comes to thinking about negotiating? We all negotiate to some extent, and in certain situations, but some only negotiate with friends and relatives. To some, the prospect of negotiating with a stranger fills them with dread. When this happens, they are simply handing victory to the other side on a plate. They not only lose the negotiation, but also the respect of the other side, and their own self-respect. You owe it to yourself to negotiate at every opportunity. You need to recognize every situation where you have enough leverage to make negotiating a sensible option. Contrary to common belief, almost everything is negotiable. Get used to using the techniques in this chapter by practicing them during less important dealings. Thus, you will be better equipped when an important negotiating opportunity comes along. However, beware of being branded a skinflint if you practice your negotiating skills on trivial matters and ultra-cheap goods that are already priced generously!

In most situations, you have some leverage

People often throw away negotiating opportunities because they don't realize they have leverage. It is important to realize that negotiating is always a two-way affair. Never assume that you naturally have the weaker hand. Don't be like the employee who meekly accepts a tiny pay rise, year after year, even though his boss values him highly. He lives with the delusion that he is so expendable, that dismissal would result if he tried to ask for higher pay. What he doesn't realize is the amount of inconvenience and expense it would cost to hire and train a replacement. Employers invariably pay employees less than they could afford to, so there is usually scope for negotiation here.

Both sides can be the winner

Surprisingly, you will often make the other party happier if you negotiate, than if you just pay the asking price. Example: You are offered a used car for $10,000. You think it's a generous offer, so you gladly pay the asking price. Does the seller then feel good? Not necessarily; he may be left feeling he should have asked a higher price. He thinks: if you were so willing to pay $10,000, you probably wouldn't have minded paying an extra $1,000. If some form of negotiation takes place, there is much more chance that a good relationship will develop, and that means potential repeated business for both sides. People respect people who negotiate—but only if they do it with sensitivity and skill. By reading this, you are already developing that skill.

Many styles of negotiating

There are many different styles of negotiating throughout the world. In Britain and America, such ploys as raised voices and angry exchanges, are usually counter-productive. The norm is to keep one's emotions in check and carefully avoid offending the other party. However, personalities do differ, and we must adapt to the other party's personality type.

The hidden factors in every negotiation

There are usually many more factors available as negotiating chips than the obvious ones. Take the employee above. Little did he know that he had certain skills that were valuable to his boss.

Price is not always the most important factor in a negotiation. There are often less obvious issues at stake and these are typically kept private. So the first task you should set yourself before entering into any important negotiation is to find out all you can about the other side. Only by doing so, can you hope to uncover those hidden factors; the things that the other party is really concerned about. In this way, you can enable the other side to get what they want, while at the same time, you get what you want in a win-win situation. This is good negotiating. Both parties come out feeling good, and mutual respect is the result.

The more you can get to know about the other side, the easier it becomes to negotiate to a win-win conclusion. This is why most people only negotiate with friends and relatives. The husband already has a very good idea of what is important to his wife. It's easy to come to an agreement that the wife can use the car this evening, as long as the husband can invite his friends over tomorrow evening.

❖ *Preparation accounts for 90% of negotiating success.*
   ---Brian Tracy

Framework for successful negotiations

The University of Kent in the UK compiled the following framework for successful negotiations:

1. Listen carefully to the arguments of the other party and assess the logic of their reasoning.
2. Clarify issues you are not clear about by asking 'how', 'why', 'where', 'when' and 'what' questions.
3. List all the issues which are important to both sides and identify the key issues.
4. Identify any personal agendas. Question generalizations and challenge assumptions.
5. Identify any areas of common ground.
6. Understand any outside forces that may be affecting the problem.
7. Keep calm and use assertive rather than aggressive behavior. Use tact and diplomacy to diffuse tensions. Remember: NO is a little word with big power!
8. Use both verbal and non-verbal persuasion skills. Use open, encouraging body language such as mirroring, not defensive or closed.
9. Know when to compromize. Offer concessions where necessary, but minor ones at first. Distinguish between needs: important points on which you can't compromise, and interests where you can concede ground. Allow the other party to save face, if necessary via small concessions.
10. Make sure there is an agreed deadline for resolution
11. Decide on a course of action and come to an agreement. The final agreement needs to be summarized and written down at the conclusion of the negotiations.
12. Plan for alternative outcomes in case you can't reach agreement.

Negotiating tactics & gambits

The following negotiating tactics are all familiar to professional negotiators. Whether or not you decide to adopt any of them for your own use, you should definitely learn about them, because they are constantly being used against you by the professionals.

The flinch

Always get the other side to be the first one to name a price. When they do, FLINCH. In other words, visibly jump with shock and exclaim "$1,500??!!" (as if to say: "Are you *serious*? I wouldn't pay *anything* like that for *this!*"). That's often enough to get the other side to drop their price substantially. Try it. Don't overdo it, but be convincing. Accentuate your exclamation exactly the right amount and it will probably work. Overdo it and you could kill the negotiation.

Generating competition

This is a common but effective ploy. For example, you say something like: "Mr X from across the road is hoping to buy it, but he doesn't finish work for another thirty minutes, and I do believe in the principle of first come, first served." If you make your client aware that someone else is poised to snatch the deal from under his nose, his desire increases dramatically.

Look for imperfections in the goods

You can often find some small fault with the goods you are considering. When you do, this is an excellent reason to negotiate a lower price. In a shop, you may have to negotiate with the manager if the assistant isn't authorized to make price reductions.

The slip of the tongue

Watch out for this one. This is where the seller tells you that his merchandise will cost you $150 a week. If you don't flinch, he knows he is onto a good thing. (He'd actually be willing to take $150 per MONTH.) If you DO flinch, and protest vehemently, he then says, "Oh, did I say $150 a week? Ha ha! How careless of me! Of course I meant $150 per MONTH! That's the general way the technique works. It is of course highly flexible and can be adapted to any situation. Another variation would be when someone says: "We want $1,600 for this item." When you start to walk out of the door in disgust, he says: "Oh, wait a minute, did I say $1,600? Stupid mistake: it is of course, $600!" Bear in mind that genuine mistakes and slips of the tongue do occur sometimes.

The nibble

You are selling your car privately. The buyer has made up his mind, and is just about to write out the check. At this moment you say: "By the way, I hope you realize the price doesn't include the roof rack and the seat covers." He's not going to change his mind now that he's so close to owning the car. When the buyer has made the decision to buy, he gets a surge of positivism. That's the moment when you spring your 'nibble'.

When used by the buyer, it goes as follows: Just as he's about to sign the check, he says something like: "By the way the price does include delivery, doesn't it?" It didn't, but the seller isn't going to risk destroying the deal by saying "no". Other nibbles you might use: asking for a full tank of petrol when you buy a car; asking for free installation when you buy a computer; asking for free collection and delivery when you get your car serviced. Always beware of the nibble that may come from your opponent. Thus you are less likely to get your hand bitten off, just as you are clinching the deal.

Always get something in return for a concession

If ever you are asked for something during negotiations, immediately ask for something in return. I say immediately because it won't wash if you leave it until later. If you can't think of anything to ask for, try saying something like: "Well, if I do that for you, what can you do for me?" It is tempting to give in and grant the concession, just to be amiable, but if you do, you'll lose the respect of the other side. He may even lose interest in the deal. If you ask for something in return for every requested concession, it conveys the impression that the item under negotiation has more value than was assumed. If you don't ask for something in return for requested concessions, it tends to erode the perceived value of the goods.

Never say "no"

Eliminate the word "no" from your vocabulary—at least when you are negotiating. It's a turn-off word. It instantly creates negative thinking, narrow-mindedness and lack of imagination. For example, let's say you are trying to sell your lawn mower to your neighbor. He asks: "Do you think you could lower your price to $175? You certainly don't want to come down that low, but whatever you do, don't say "no". The word "no" as a response is almost an insult. It means you can't even be bothered to reciprocate your neighbor's attempt to negotiate a mutually acceptable price. Don't make "no" the first word of your response. Try instead: "Well, I'll have to think about that." Or: "I'd like to help, but if I came down that low, I'd lose out." I think you get the idea. In fact you should try to eliminate nearly all negative words, as they generate negativity and kill creativity and open-mindedness.

Learn to think on your feet

If there is one area of life where it pays to be quick-witted it is the negotiation arena. A split-second delay in spotting a good negotiating gambit can spell big losses. Saying the wrong thing or missing an opportunity tend to be mistakes that are hard to make up for. One ill-considered comment can kill the deal completely. It is best to be wide awake and in top form, so prepare for each negotiating session in every way you can.

In negotiating situations, always try to create a 'positive response atmosphere'. Make the other side feel good about themselves and avoid arguing, interrupting or contradicting. However, do not be afraid to ask questions. And remember to observe body language. It can often betray your opponent's true thoughts and feelings. See the chapter on this subject.

Good negotiating should result in mutual liking and respect; never in ill-will. This is the hallmark of a skilled negotiator. Unskilled negotiating is just trying to get the best deal for oneself, without any thought for the other side's needs.

RECOMMENDED ACTION STEP

Practice and develop your negotiating skills at every opportunity where negotiating could benefit you. Most things in life are negotiable to some extent, and most people don't bother to try negotiating as much as they could. By taking the opportunity to negotiate over small issues regularly, you can become much better equipped when you next have to negotiate over some really big and important issue. However, do remember that not every situation demands the same negotiating style. Your negotiating style should suit the occasion. Keep a record in your A-Log about any new negotiating insights you pick up during these practice sessions.

21
AN ENTERPRISE OF YOUR OWN
COULD THIS BE FOR YOU?

❖ *Correct observation followed by meticulous deduction and the precise visualization of goals is vital to the success of any enterprise.* —Terry Pratchett

With an enterprise of your own, everything you do is aimed at making you more successful. If you work for someone else, everything you do for them is aimed at making *them* more successful. The self-made millionaires of the world achieved their wealth through successful enterprise. Could an enterprise of your own be the best way forward for you? This chapter will help you decide.

There are many paths to wealth in this life. Some are more commendable than others. You could marry a billionaire, sit around indefinitely, hoping that you'll win the lottery, or plan to burgle Fort Knox. The last one could be particularly foolhardy, since no-one seems certain whether there is any gold left inside Fort Knox!

There's another way!

It could be much more satisfying and profitable in the long run to start a business doing something you enjoy doing. Self-employment is not for everyone. Some prefer regular employment because it requires less thought and planning and perhaps less responsibility.

If you decide on self-employment and the small enterprise path, you don't have to jump in at the deep end of the pool; you can start off making money in your spare time.

There is much to be said for starting your own business, doing what you believe in and enjoy. You have much more say in the direction of your life, and it may earn you greater respect and self-respect. And ultimately, you could end up richer, if you plan with due forethought. If you think this could be your path to fulfillment, then there is no time like the present to make preparations to get started.

Even if your first attempt is not as successful as you hoped, all is not lost; you'll have gained valuable experience for your next enterprise. Even if money is not your prime motive, there's nothing quite as satisfying as being your own boss, in a field of work that you enjoy.

There's no substitute for experience

People spend a lot of money and time gaining a business education, and still don't get out there and actually get started. Once you have a basic grounding in business, perhaps by attending a free government enterprise scheme, there is no experience quite as valuable as taking the plunge and doing something. It does take courage, and you may start to question your faith in yourself at the critical moment. However, it is by overcoming challenges that you build your self-confidence. So set yourself small achievable goals, conquer them, and move on up. Remember the old saying: "Inch by inch, everything is a cinch."

Pick the right business for you

Think very carefully about what line of business you want to get into. Anticipate being tied to this line of work for ten or more years, so you must think carefully about your own temperament and psychological make-up when deciding. For instance, which of the following do you most enjoy working with? (a) people, (b) data, (c) things.

Since you will be spending a large percentage of your time working on your chosen business, in order to be successful, it is extremely important to choose something that you are going to enjoy. If you do not already know what you enjoy most, think back on your life and consider which types of productive activity you have indulged in, where the hours seem to disappear, and you find yourself wondering where the last few hours went.

Be different, be daring, and be first

You will stand a much greater chance of success if you avoid ideas that are already commonplace. To come up with an original idea you need to be truly creative. How do you perfect your creative idea? You simply work on it. Keep refining it. Then when it shines, you can unleash it. There is something spiritual and irresistible about creativity. Everyone has it. You just need to find the avenue of creativity that you feel you could happily become involved with as a way of life for the next few years. You may never come up with the perfect business idea, so if you are still unsure after deliberating for a reasonable period, perhaps you should settle for one of your less-than-perfect ideas. It might be better to run a less-than-perfect business than none at all.

Whatever field of business you take up, you'll have to make your service more attractive than that of your competitors in some way. This is known as your USP (unique selling point). This is worth some careful and creative thinking.

Pre-plan an escape route

Try to leave yourself an escape route in case things don't work out as expected. Try and settle for an idea that gives you some scope for a change of direction. Planning will pay off here. Don't get locked into an inescapable rut.

Don't expect to get rich overnight

Money may not, of course, be your prime reason for wanting your own business. But if it is, remember that many multi-million-dollar businesses started off as part-time 'kitchen table' ventures. If you are patient, and stick at it, without making any silly mistakes, you can expect salary increases far greater than any you could as an employee.

Most people give up too quickly when they discover they are not making as much as expected. But it's not so much how much you can make, as how steadily, and at what rate your income increases over the months. Therefore, buy some large sheets of graph paper, pin them up along the wall of your office. Up the right-hand margin of the far left piece, mark off dollars in hundreds or thousands, and along the bottom margin write in the months of the year as from the current month. Every month, mark on it the month's takings. There will probably be some fluctuations, but if after a few months, you can see a definite upward trend in the figures, you may, after careful consideration, conclude that if you just hang in there and keep working at it, you will eventually realize your financial dreams.

Take stock of your assets

Material assets

These include money, property, tools of your trade, etc. Do you have special access to a product or a raw material that you could sell, or turn into something that you could sell? Is there going to be an ongoing supply of this commodity—enough to supply your business in weeks, months, or years to come?

Non-material assets

These include your skills, talents, knowledge, creativity, and contacts. To get a head start in your business venture, you'll want to be able to make maximum use of your assets. It is your own unique combination of assets that gives you your special chance to succeed.

Look to the future

Will your type of service or merchandise be in demand in years to come? You must be objective when working out your answer to this one. Gather all the hard facts you can from as many sources as possible. Even go out with a clipboard, a list of questions and a pen, and do your own market research. Whatever it takes, get those hard facts. It can easily mean the difference between success and failure. Most business ventures fail simply because this question was never properly asked. Simple logical thinking is a good place to start. The goods and services that will be in demand in coming years can be predicted to some extent by certain trends that are taking place now. So identify all the trends you can think of. For example:

- the rapid development and public availability of computer technology
- the increase in trade between the nations of Europe
- the economic rise of South East Asia
- the rise in the crime rate
- the increasing amounts of leisure time people are experiencing
- the ever-worsening traffic congestion
- the rapidly increasing population and the resulting effects

Only by looking at trends can we can hope to predict what tomorrow's customers will be willing to pay for. List all the trends you can think of.

Will you sell goods or a service?

If you take up business studies, you will soon learn that service businesses usually stand a better chance of succeeding than retail businesses. When you are manufacturing or selling material goods, you are wide open to competition. People with greater capital resources than you will be able to undercut your prices, because they are able to save money by buying stock in larger quantities. As just one example, look at the small shops that have been put out of business by the arrival of large supermarkets in their neighborhood. You'll also be subject to competition from overseas importers. Other countries are often able to produce goods cheaper than we can. In particular, think twice before embarking on any type of retail business where you have to pay for stock before you can resell it. This requires skilful financial control to avoid disaster.

Look ahead, long-term

When selecting a business of your own, it's important to think ahead and envisage what life will be like in, say, ten or even twenty years' time. Does what you see reflect the kind of life you will be happy living? The chances are that if your business gets off the ground, you will be stuck with it for the long haul. That's why it is a good idea to make sure it's something that gives you a lot of satisfaction—something that you won't get tired of easily.

Commit to quality, right from the start

Get the habit of quality right from the word go. That is quality of service, and if you're going to manufacture or sell goods, quality of goods also. Committing to quality right from the start is much easier than trying to do it after you've developed habits of sloppiness. Quality of image is another important factor. Customers tend to form an opinion of a business by what they see first. That could be your stationery, your advertising, your shop front or you. Be sure to create a first impression of quality. Have a good look at how other quality businesses present themselves, to get some ideas.

Office equipment

If you haven't done so already, get computerized. Most people are these days, but it's surprising how many still aren't taking full advantage of the technology. Resist at all costs, however, the powerful temptation to spend any more than you need to on computers, software and business equipment. This temptation is a common stumbling block among new enterprises. If you look carefully, you may well find that a machine that serves your needs can be bought for half the price of the latest and greatest machines that the dealers would love you to buy. The owners find themselves with available credit, and decide to spoil themselves. It's a common root cause of failure in business. Hopefully, you will get so much satisfaction from the kind of work you are involved with, that you won't feel the urge to buy any business 'toys' that are beyond your basic needs. Beware of the salesmen, and the free offers that come in the mail. They will try every trick in the book to convince you that you need more than you already have. Buy only the equipment that will quickly enable you to increase your profits.

Do you have the know-how yet?

Not only will you need some basic know-how, but you will also need a burst of self-confidence and courage. Know-how comes first though. So make the decision right now to start studying the important basics of business. You will of course need to know more than most people about your chosen line of business. Running a business is largely a matter of common sense. However, do familiarize yourself with the following key subjects:

Business studies

This is a subject widely taught in evening classes. If you sign up, you'll get the opportunity to discuss your grey areas with knowledgeable people. The subject gives you an important grounding in the way business works. It will enable you to see the big picture.

Selling & negotiating

These are two vital skills you won't typically learn about in business studies classes and books. Did you ever wonder why people who graduate in business studies generally don't go into business and succeed at it? It's because they didn't learn these fundamental skills!

Money

Find out all you can about lending, borrowing, inflation, investment, banking, taxation, economics and how money works.

Public relations

Every organization depends on its reputation for its success. A good reputation can be a company's most important asset. To excel in PR, a person needs good verbal and written communication skills, so if you (or your PR person) don't possess these aptitudes yet, now is the time to start looking for ways to improve them. PR courses at many levels of complexity are available for those who seek them out.

Book-keeping and cash flow forecasting

Book-keeping and cash-flow forecasting are about financial planning. These tools are your headlights; they light up the road ahead. Many businesses fail, simply because their owners never learned how to see ahead. They don't plan to fail; they simply fail to plan! You wouldn't take a drive on a dark night without headlights, would you? The same applies to business. Managing a business is much the same as driving a car or sailing a boat. Plan your journey at all stages, and you are less likely to hit a lamp post, run out of gas, or capsize in stormy waters.

Overcome the obstacles

You may decide that you are hopelessly uninformed or unskilled in some area considered vital for business people. For instance, you may be hopeless with figures, or at dealing with people. Do all you can to overcome these deficiencies. Live by the belief that you can learn anything if you simply take things one step at a time. If you have a genuinely insurmountable handicap, still don't give up! There is always a way to overcome. Remember you can always enlist the help of others.

Business partnerships

Business partnerships are notorious for failing, and the resulting legal tangles are often horrendous. Often, one partner starts to feel that he or she is being exploited by the other one, yet they are locked in a relationship they can't easily get out of. If you are considering someone as a partner, could you perhaps employ him for a year first? If you must have a partner, make it is someone you know well, and make sure it someone with complementary skills to your own. Choosing a partner with the same skills as you is a wasted opportunity. For most people, life is far more satisfying being one's own boss, not having to answer to anyone else.

Don't give up

Overcome those setbacks and obstacles. Turn them into advantages if you can. Every cloud has a silver lining. If things start to look daunting, and you get twinges of pessimism, just take a rest from it; the mind tends to think negatively when it is tired. Never panic. If you do, you will make rash, impulsive decisions.

❖ *Never, never, never give up!* —Winston Churchill

Devotion

You stand the best chance of succeeding (possibly your only chance) if you devote most of your time and thinking to your business venture. If your situation requires that you maintain regular employment, try to make sure it is a job that helps your business venture in some way; for instance: one that either gives you the experience you need or the contacts you need. If your job doesn't require all your attention, you may be able to devote some of your attention to your business idea while you work. If your job involves driving, you might be able to play tutorial tapes in the car. If it involves periods of waiting, you can grasp the chance to read up on your chosen subjects.

Success

Successful is the person who loves his work, and has found a way to use his or her talents to provide a service to the community. Success is more about how much you can offer than about how much money you can make. Seek continuously to improve the quality of service you can offer.

Be customer oriented! That is to say, look after your customers. Satisfy them (but not so much that they don't need to come back to you for more)! Make every effort to find out what they want, how they want it, why they want it, when they want it and where they want it. Find out what your customers think about the quality of your service, and your prices. Customer questionnaires can provide you with this information. Too many businesses never bother to find out what their customers want. They think they already know, and the penalty for such folly is usually to get beaten by the competition. It happens all the time.

❖ *Be true to what naturally interests you—and be brave enough to turn an obsession into a profession.*
   —Shelly Branch

❖ *Chase the vision, not the money; the money will end up following you. —Tony Hsieh Zappos*

❖ *Empty pockets never held anyone back. Only empty heads and empty hearts can do that. —Norman Vincent Peale*

- *Your work is going to fill a large part of your life, and the only way to be truly satisfied is to do what you believe is great work. And the only way to do great work is to love what you do. —Steve Jobs*

- *If you don't build your dream. Someone will hire you to help build theirs. —Tony Gaskins*

RECOMMENDED ACTION STEP

Consider whether a business venture of some kind could be a way to further your ultimate life goals. If this might be the case, start making a list of your skills and assets that could give you a key advantage. Do you have any ardent enthusiasms or obsessions that could be turned into a business venture – even if only a part-time one?

If you think you have the makings of a plan, take plenty of time and spare no effort in researching the potentiality of your idea as a viable business. Enthusiasm alone is definitely NOT the magic ingredient that ensures success.

Be very careful about other people's ready-made business plans which they have hyped up to sound like golden opportunities, when they are really only golden opportunities for someone else to profit from your investment of time, money and effort.

PART FOUR

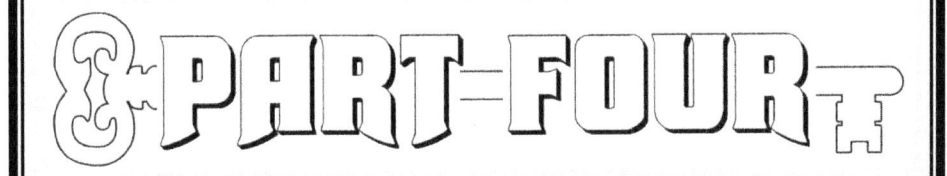

FORMIDABLE FORMULAS FOR FASTER FULFILLMENT

We have likened this program to a formidable flying machine. It can keep you flying high and straight and with remarkable progress while competing aircraft frequently veer off course - often into prohibited airspace, conflict zones, or stormy weather. Others fall to earth, having spent their fuel prematurely.

You have in your possession the best flight plan for your unique needs, and the best compass, aviation charts and flying instructions. Your flying machine comes supplied with a special selection of advanced training documents that you can read and absorb while cruising aloft. These will diversify and augment your flying skills tremendously. Through these, you will be better equipped to take best advantage of every situation fate can throw at you, and each of the following chapters is a place you can land and take on board vital fuel and provisions!

❖ *Who shall set a limit to the influence of a human being?*
  —Ralph Waldo Emerson

22
DAVID & GOLIATH PRINCIPLE
LESS EFFORT, BETTER RESULTS!

❖ *Give me a lever long enough and a fulcrum on which to place it, and I shall move the world." —Archimedes*

By concentrating one's efforts where it counts the most, one can often achieve great things with surprisingly little effort, as expressed in the above quote on leverage. This chapter looks at this key strategy and reveals how you can apply the David and Goliath (D&G) principle for seismic results!

In the famous Bible story, the boy David succeeds in defeating his opponent, the giant Goliath. How? Goliath was probably clad in armor and all David had for a weapon was a sling and a small stone. He simply used this key tactic! To seal Goliath's fate, he focused his efforts on a single strategic key point (his opponent's unprotected forehead). Most people never become successful because they don't consider this principle. They fritter away their daily efforts without focusing on the key points that would bring the best results. Let's see how this principle can be applied.

In everyday life

Every time you are faced with a problem, write down its key factors. Often, you can easily solve complex problems just by tackling the first one or two items on your list. Use a similar technique each night when planning your schedule for the following day. Every night, write down the few most important tasks you must carry out the next day, bearing in mind your long-term and short-term goals. By focusing your best efforts on the key factors, you immediately become more effective.

In business

In business, it is often held that the best strategy is to diversify, offering a wide range of services or products, to a broad range of customers. This is a tempting strategy, but usually a foolish one. In business, your attention should be focused on narrow, well-defined target groups of customers. This way, you can realistically become a market leader, and the market leader gets the custom. Most people would find it more rewarding to be number one in a small field of business than to be one of many contenders in a large one. So focus on your most promising target group of customers, then focus on that group's main problems and work out how your own, or your company's, greatest strengths can solve them. Businesses that employ this strategy most often succeed.

Get the most from your customer base

A mistake commonly made in business is to invest too much in gaining new customers, and not enough in keeping the existing ones. Most businesses can easily increase their annual revenue substantially by applying the D&G principle to their existing customers. Analyze your customer base in terms of how much they spend on your goods and services. The chances are, you'll find that about 20% of them are providing about 80% of your revenues. So it makes sense to invest some of your resources in keeping this select minority happy.

When speculating and investing

Again, the usual advice is: "Spread the risk." Good advice—if you want poor returns; you end up with virtually no risk and consequently poor prospect of gains. Instead, consider applying the D&G Principle: Do your research thoroughly, until you find the small number of investments that look most promising, then make a major investment in them. Minimize the risk by doing your research thoroughly.

When dealing with organizations

When dealing with organizations, it is essential to learn who is the best person to negotiate with. Take the time to find out who is the key person to deal with. It must be the person who has the authority to adjust the price, give the command, influence the committee, place the order, etc. Tremendous expense is wasted every day by people who aren't wise to this.

To capitalize on your skills

By deploying your greatest skills, you stand the best chance of being competitive, having the most to offer, or gaining the highest salary. If you run a business, try to apply your best skills to your business, and think about how you can apply them to solving the problems of your most important group of clients. When tasks arise for which you don't have the necessary skills, delegate those tasks to the people best qualified to tackle them.

When taking notes

You may occasionally need to take notes quickly, for example at an important lecture, or during a TV program. Rather than scribble away frantically trying to capture everything on paper, just write down a few key words, or mental triggers. This way you leave a good portion of your attention free to absorb and understand what's being said. You can rewrite your notes in full later if necessary.

When tackling problems

How can you apply this key success secret today? What is the main problem hanging over your life? What is the main key obstacle standing between you and perfect happiness? Now, what is the single most important aspect of that problem—the area on which you should concentrate your best effort for optimum effect? Can you deploy your most powerful skills in solving this problem? Write down all the areas in your life where you can apply the D&G principle. Use every effort to focus on the key issue; then act.

RECOMMENDED ACTION STEP

In your A-Log, list all the matters in your life where the D&G principle can be applied. Note down how you can be more effective by focusing your efforts on the small but key areas that really matter. For example, if you run a business, see if you can identify the small percentage of your customers that account for most of your revenues. What can you do to make those particular customers extra happy and inclined to want more of your goods or services?

❖ *By prevailing over all obstacles and distractions, one may unfailingly arrive at his chosen goal or destination.*
—Christopher Columbus

23
AVOIDING DISTRACTIONS
THE IMPEDIMENT TO PROGRESS

❖ *It's a great deal. Just put on some earmuffs and you become 5-10% smarter. —Peter Rogers*

Distractions proliferate wherever we go. Some people are so consumed by the distractions of life that they have entirely lost sight of any sense of purpose. Don't be one of them; claim back your soul and get back on track for the really meaningful rewards that will make a real difference to your life.

What is the primary foe of the earnest seeker of self-fulfillment? Answer: Distractions! Distractions are like vampires. They can gorge on your precious time and would gladly hijack your soul, commandeer your life and gobble up your attention. Let us start with one of the arch-vampires of modern life: television!

Television - the arch culprit!

Statistics reveal that the average citizen of the Western world watches more than five hours of television a day at the time of this writing. That's about a third of their waking hours - or a third of their waking life! That is an awfully large percentage of a life to donate to a lump of metal and plastic that seeks to keep you hypnotized so it can program you with all kinds of rubbish that is of no benefit to you, but is only of benefit to the programmers.

It is true that not all of what we see on TV is useless garbage, but a large proportion of it is just programming designed to make money from you while giving you practically nothing useful in return. In fact a large proportion of what you receive in return for complying with these devices for profiting from your attention is contrary to your best interests. While you sit, hypnotized, you are absorbing a vast amount of programming, conditioning and brainwashing, and taking on board other people's attitudes, opinions, beliefs, mental habits, and attitudes, many of which are far from healthy or beneficial. How could it be, when the makers of the programs don't even know you?

❖ *I must say I find television very educational. The minute somebody turns it on, I go into the library and read a good book.* —Groucho Marx

Even the programs that most people think of as purely informative and educative often have some kind of political slant or agenda that promote the interest of the program makers and their production companies. Corporate news media in particular, while careful not to seem blatantly biased, all have an agenda, be it conscious or subconscious, for shaping public opinion. Most of them are carefully censored and modified to keep you from considering viewpoints that don't further their interests, or the interests of the puppeteers who pull their strings.

❖ *If you came and you found a strange man... teaching your kids to punch each other, or trying to sell them all kinds of products, you'd kick him right out of the house, but here you are; you come in and the TV is on, and you don't think twice about it.* —Jerome Singer

Life is short

Life is short and time is precious. You only get one chance to make the most of it. Imagine for a moment you had a car accident and your vital organs had been irreparably damaged. The hospital surgeon gives you the grim news: you will be dead within the next 12 hours. How much would you pay to have a life extension of 16 years? My guess is that you'd willingly give everything you own for that reprieve, yes? Sixteen years is about the total time the average person spends watching TV during their lifetime!

Second-hand life!

You may be thinking: "But hang on! I get pleasure from television! That counts for something, doesn't it?" Agreed, that does have *some* value - but *only some, and often at a cost!* There is perhaps some value in TV when used for your own calculated purposes, and in suitable amounts. But the thing to understand is that most people watch TV to get enjoyable feelings. They only need to do that because they are not getting those feelings from real life. Television is not real life; it's second-hand life, or imaginary life. Wouldn't you rather get all the positive feelings you need from REAL life? Television's pleasures are ALWAYS a substitute for the real thing. People watch soaps and movies and suchlike to fill the gaps and deficiencies in their own life. And ultimately, they risk becoming brain-dead vegetables!

Watching TV trains you *not* to think for yourself. You definitely don't need TV to be happy; you would be far better off learning to use your own mind to derive happiness from real life, through your own self-programming—not the programming of nameless people who don't even know you, and don't care much about what's in your best interests.

If you are planning and living your own life optimally, you simply won't have time for TV and other wasteful distractions. If you have identified your true calling and have a vision of your own ultimate fulfillment and are taking all the necessary steps to achieve it, you will be getting an abundance of positive emotions such as hope and exhilaration from real life, and you'll see TV and other distractions for what they really are: mental vampires! You'll find that there simply aren't enough hours in the day to waste any of them on television or any other pursuits that are not chosen primarily to advance you to your own exciting objectives. Your true comfort zone will not be sitting in front of the TV but will be actively making progress towards your ultimate goals and ambitions.

Other hazards of watching too much television

Besides the manipulative and unhelpful programming to which you subject yourself when watching TV, there are other ways that television is detrimental. A lot of the most seductive and adrenaline-producing programs are broadcast after 9 pm. That's roughly the time when we should be starting the process of winding down, and preparing for an early night of deep and restful sleep. Medical experts tell us that, as a rule of thumb, we need around seven to nine hours of sleep a night for optimal recuperation. When we start the process of winding down in the evening and indeed while we are sleeping, our minds engage in the all-important process of digesting and processing all of the things we have experienced during the day. Much of this happens at a subconscious level but it goes on just the same. If you start burdening the mind with extra stuff to digest and process—such as TV movies, anxiety-producing TV news, or any other stimulating or disturbing input, you will overload your subconscious mind with stuff that is probably not even of any importance to your primary objectives. The result is that you wake up the following day without having fully digested and assimilated everything that needs digesting, and consequently, you won't be optimally happy and effective.

The same thing happens when you over-engage in social activity in the evenings. Every time you do so, you will be taking on board a lot of the psychological and emotional problems of those people you interact with.

There are many other time-consuming distractions

TV is only one of the numerous distractions that are vying to hold your attention and keep you from advancing towards your own true self-fulfillment and true happiness. Think of all the other similar distractions: radio, newspapers, idle gossip, time-wasting pastimes and everything else that is not something you've deliberately chosen to increase the rapidity with which you can attain your key objectives and make progress towards your own true self-fulfillment!

Many people are news junkies. We even see them watching the same news headlines repeatedly, several times a day. Keeping abreast of current events has its benefits, but the self-empowered success-seeker will typically scan the headlines of newspapers once a day, but won't get hooked into delving further into any news which does not have any immediate bearing on his life and personal program.

❖ *If you dream of something worth doing and then simply go to work on it and don't think anything of personalities, or emotional conflicts, or of money, or of family distractions; it is amazing how quickly you get through those 5,000 steps.*
—Edwin Land

RECOMMENDED ACTION STEP

Become aware of how much of your time you are wasting, seduced by other people's self-interested desire to use up your time, including TV programming, newspapers, magazines, idle gossip and other pastimes that you haven't specifically and intentionally chosen to advance you towards your ultimate ambitions. Keep a notebook with you and record the time you spend on such activities every day.

❖ *It has been my observation that most people get ahead during the time that others waste.* —Henry Ford

24
THE IRREPLACEABLE ASSET
AND HOW TO USE IT

❖ *Dost thou love life? Then do not squander time, for that is the stuff life is made of.* —Benjamin Franklin

If time is our most valuable asset, it follows that we should invest it wisely. Let's consider how we can make the best use of it. Once it has been spent, it cannot be replaced. This chapter looks at this in detail and reveals ways we can invest time wisely.

Time is an equal opportunity employer; each human being has exactly the same number of hours and minutes every day! Rich people can't buy more hours. Concentrate your best efforts and your prime time to the matters that really count. It is a good idea, to spend a little time each night deciding which of the following day's tasks are most important. It's a very good policy to write down these most important tasks and rank each according to its importance.

Observe Parkinson's Law

Parkinson's Law states: ***"Work expands to fill the time available for its completion,"*** i.e. "The thing to be done expands in importance and complexity in direct ratio with the time allocated to it." You can get more done by allocating less time for tasks. You'll often find that working to a tight deadline forces you to work much more efficiently. The work then becomes more challenging and exciting too.

How are you spending your time?

Keeping a time log for a week or two has some remarkable benefits. You'll discover activities that have been surreptitiously eating up your time. You'll get a good idea of how long your different tasks usually take. This will enable you to plan ahead much more effectively. As soon as you wake up in the morning, start recording all your activities until the day ends.

What is your time worth?

Figures based on a person working 260 eight-hour days per year.
The figures can be dollars, pounds, or whatever currency applies to you.

Annual Income	Each day is worth	One hour is worth	1 hour a day for 260 days is worth
10,000	38.46	4.81	1,250
12,000	46.15	5.77	1,500
14,000	53.85	6.73	1,750
16,000	61.54	7.69	2,000
18,000	69.23	8.65	2,250
20,000	76.92	9.62	2,500
25,000	96.15	12.02	3,125
30,000	115.38	14.42	3,750
35,000	134.62	16.83	4,375
40,000	153.85	19.23	5,000
45,000	173.08	21.63	5,625
50,000	192.31	24.04	6,250
55,000	211.54	26.44	6,875
60,000	230.77	28.85	7,500
65,000	250.00	31.25	8,125
70,000	269.23	33.65	8,750
75,000	288.46	36.06	9,375
80,000	307.69	38.46	10,000
85,000	326.92	40.87	10,625
90,000	346.15	43.27	11,250
95,000	365.38	45.67	11,875
100,000	384.62	48.08	12,500
120,000	461.54	57.69	15,000
140,000	538.46	67.31	17,500
160,000	615.38	76.92	20,000
180,000	692.31	86.54	22,500
200,000	769.23	96.15	25,000

Don't save minutes and waste hours!

Just as you should avoid looking after the pennies while throwing away the dollars, you should avoid being 'minute-wise but hour-foolish'. Also beware of combining the two: saving pennies, but wasting hours as a consequence. One example is the person who spends half an hour walking to another shop so he can buy an item a few pence cheaper. Another is the person who travels by bus instead of by air, because it's a few dollars cheaper, but ignores the fact that it takes three times as long. Again, it helps if you have an idea of what your time is worth in dollars per hour.

DIY or delegate?

Every time you consider embarking on a task or project, stop to consider whether the work you're planning is worth your while. Will it bring returns greater than the value of the time you are investing, or should you delegate or pay someone else to do it, thereby freeing up your time, so you can use it in more profitable ways? Use the table to look up the value of your time. The table applies to people who work eight hours a day, 260 days a year. The figures can be in dollars, pounds, or whatever currency applies to you.

Stratagems to adopt

Do two things at once

Do two things at the same time, as long as neither of them requires your full attention. By doing so you can make more time for yourself. Sort those papers while watching the News. Tidy up your workspace while you talk on the telephone. Listen to educational tapes while driving, etc.

Do some work when you can't sleep

Do you suffer from insomnia or wake up too early? Why not get up and do some work. It doesn't have to be anything too demanding. In fact it makes excellent sense to do your trivial jobs when you are not in tip-top mental condition. Do demanding jobs during the time of day when you are at your mental and physical peak.

A place for everything

Avoid wasting time hunting around for mislaid items. The secret is to have a place for everything, and to train yourself to put everything back in its allocated place after you've finished using it. Always look before you leap. It is at those times when you leap without looking that you are most likely to forget to put something in its proper place. For example, you realize that the last mail collection goes in ten minutes, so you drop everything and dash to your car. Just a few seconds spent recapping where everything is placed, and what stage your work is at before you dash off will pay rich rewards.

Learn how to interrupt

Learn the art of interrupting people. If you master it, you can do it without offending the other side, and you'll save yourself from having to hear out volumes of verbiage that you have no need for. Learn to interrupt the person who's speaking to you, but also learn to butt into other people's conversations. Do this for example, to procure information, when you need it quickly.

Avoid conflict

Avoid conflict wherever possible. Arguments, disagreements, and especially court cases, all gobble up time.

The winner in such conflicts is often the loser in terms of lost time and lost money. Learn the art of avoiding conflict. Be willing to make concessions and reach a compromize instead. If you are emotionally distraught by a recent altercation, your mind will be in no fit state to work effectively. You'll make mistakes and be very inefficient. The only way to get the best of an argument is to avoid it.

Save time only if there's good reason to

Many people today tend to do everything in a rush because they are obsessed with saving time. But what do they do with the time they save? They waste it! It makes sense to always consider the best ways you can use the time you are trying to save.

Take time off regularly

Take time off work. Centuries ago, farmers knew that if they left a field uncultivated for the whole growing season once every four years, it would produce more crops in the long run. Exactly the same applies to you and your work, and to your thinking. If you try to plod on day after day, seven days a week, your productivity will fall. Take regular time off. You'll be giving your subconscious mind a chance to digest everything it has been taking in, while you give your conscious mind a rest.

Do things at unusual times

If you do things when everyone else is doing them, what happens? Here is what happens:

- You get stuck in traffic jams.
- You have to endure queues.
- You don't get quality service.

- You have to make an appointment.
- You can't get a decent table in the restaurant.
- You have to pay top dollar for your holidays, then find the beach is overcrowded.
- You can't buy the ideal Xmas presents because they've all been sold.

Supertime and Golden Core activities

Supertime is the name we can use for time that has the maximum payoff in relation to time spent. As a general rule, you can categorize all activities into four classes or levels. The four quarters in the diagram show how we identify each level of activity.

	Urgent	Not urgent
Important	Level 1 tasks	GOLDEN CORE Level 4 Tasks
Not important	Level 2 tasks	Level 3 tasks

Level 1 tasks: important and urgent
Level 2 tasks: not important but still urgent
Level 3 tasks: neither important nor urgent
Level 4 GOLDEN CORE tasks: important but not urgent

Activities that fall into section No.4 have potentially the highest pay-off in relation to time invested.

Things that need doing tend to have a deadline by which they must be done if they are to result in some payoff or reward. The closer we get to that deadline, the more urgent the task or activity becomes. Also, the closer we get to the deadline, the less time we have to carry out the activity to optimal effect and the more we will be under pressure from the rapidly approaching deadline. Such pressures undermine our ability to carry out the activity to the best of our ability.

Ineffective people devote most of their time to activities under levels 1, 2, and 3, and tend to ignore level 4 tasks. Even experienced managers often operate at a fraction of their potential, because they tend to put things off until they become urgent. They consequently spend most of their time doing activities that are important and urgent. Consequently they never have time to do the most important activities as effectively as they could. They mistakenly think that level 4 activities are not important until they become urgent, and so, when they aren't muddling through trying to take care of urgent activities, they may well waste time on activities that are neither important nor urgent.

People who understand the concept of SUPERTIME and GOLDEN CORE tasks (level 4) devote as much time as they can to these Golden Core (level 4) activities. The sooner you get started on these important activities, even though they aren't yet urgent, the more scope there is to do them well, and thus maximize their pay-off potential. Because you aren't under any serious pressure to complete them, you have more creativity at your disposal. You will probably enjoy them more as well. If you make a mistake, there's plenty of time to correct it without coming unstuck. Tasks can be done more smoothly and quickly if they are done before they become urgent. A looming deadline is a source of anxiety which is detrimental to calm concentration. Tasks carried out in a state of panic frequently end up taking twice as long, yet with a result that's only half as effective!

- *Time is the most valuable thing a man can spend.*
  —Theophrastus

- *The more business a man has to do, the more he is able to accomplish, for he learns to economize his time.*
  —Sir Matthew Hal

- *One today is worth two tomorrows.* —Benjamin Frankli

RECOMMENDED ACTION STEPS

1) For seven days, on paper, keep a careful track of how you spend your waking hours. You may well be startled by how much of your time could be put to better uses that would advance the materialization of your important goals.

2) In your A-Log, keep a running list of ways you can save time, or divert time to more beneficial uses.

3) Categorize all the tasks on your to-do list according to the four levels of task we have discussed. Identify where you can devote more time to Level 4 Golden Core tasks.

❖ *Love is that splendid triggering of human vitality the supreme activity which nature affords anyone for going out of himself toward someone else.* —José Ortega y Gasset

25
IMPROVING VITALITY
FOR INCREASED EFFECTIVENESS

❖ *The inner fire is the most important thing mankind possesses.* —Edith Södergran

Even if you have been following the advice of this book with intent diligence, you could still suffer from the handicap of inadequate energy and vitality. You may find yourself too exhausted after your day's work to think effectively about developing your goals and your affirmations, solving your problems with the Pyramid Plan Situation Transformer, or planning goal-oriented activities. The more energy you have, the more easily you can achieve your goals.

It goes without saying that the first thing to ensure is that your diet is healthy and that you aren't consuming any more dubious chemicals and drugs (including alcohol) than you need to. It also helps to maintain a good degree of physical exercise. A brisk 30-minute walk every day has tremendous benefits on your general health and wellbeing. It is also helpful to drink a good amount of water each day.

With the obvious things out of the way, let us now look at some of the less obvious ones—the things that many people overlook.

Improve your mood; improve your energy

Every word you think and speak has some electrochemical reaction in your body. Every word connected with your fears and worries triggers the release of the hormones of fear in your body. Every word you think and speak connected with your greatest emotions and hopes triggers the release of the hormones of happiness. Certain words can uplift your mood and increase your energy! Words like **fantastic, amazing, fabulous, brilliant, adorable, sublime, awesome, phenomenal, ecstatic, tremendous, outstanding, divine, beautiful, heavenly** and many others actually uplift your mind and body. Make a list of all such words you can think of and then make a point of using them at every opportunity and see how you energy levels improve! Let us now consider some things that can deplete our vitality.

Nervous tension

A moderate amount of stress and nervous tension is good; it improves our performance. If we don't get enough of it, we slow down and lose motivation. Too much of it over a sustained period however, will deplete our energies and wear us down. Nervous tension is created when stress hormones are secreted into the blood by the adrenal glands. This is the body's natural response to perceived danger. It's a biochemical boost that gives us increased potential for a fight or a flight. In modern life however, these hormones can often be more of a hindrance than a help. In the days when man was still primitive, he behaved like other animals. When frightened, he would automatically convert his adrenaline into energy, usually by fleeing from something, or by engaging in combat. Running away was the healthier option (assuming it resulted in escape from danger). Running converts adrenaline to energy as fast as it can be produced (and of course it is great aerobic exercise).

The problem for modern man is that the 'fight or flight' response is usually no longer appropriate. For example, a man's boss makes him angry at work. What can he do to burn up that adrenaline? He can't punch him and run away! Instead he has to suppress his natural inclination to fight or flee, so his adrenaline lingers in his blood causing unproductive muscular tension and nervousness. Driving home, still wound up by the experience, he has a minor collision with another car, whose driver stops, jumps out, and approaches him, shouting abuse. Again, his adrenaline levels rise. Life is full of little threats which raise our adrenaline levels. A constant excess of adrenaline in the blood drains our vitality and prevents us from operating in a cool, calm, objective way. Therefore it is vital to know how to banish it from our systems. Vigorous physical exercise, deep breathing, deep relaxation and stretching exercises are all effective.

Vigorous physical exercise is excellent for purging the body of unwanted tensions. It frees up our energies. Exercising also produces hormones that counteract negative or depressed states of mind. If you're not used to exercising, start your regular exercise program gently. Intensify it gradually as the days pass. It will take a few days for you really to start enjoying the rewards.

Staying relaxed in tense situations

Remember those important occasions when you felt tense and nervous. Your tension may even have ruined the situation for you. Perhaps it was an important interview, or were you called upon to make a speech? Perhaps you had to talk your way out of an encounter with a policeman who accused you of a traffic offence.

In all these situations, staying calm and relaxed would be very helpful. If you know the event is coming in advance, avoid drinks containing caffeine for at least twelve hours preceding the event. When the event is upon you, you can counteract nervous tension by taking deep breaths and using the following method: Intentionally tense up one group of muscles as hard as you can, and sustain it for as long as you can. This will burn up a lot of the nervous energy that is causing the tension. If you are in public view, this can still be done effectively if you make it a group of muscles that are out of sight. All of these will do the trick: pulling in your stomach hard, tensioning your buttocks, forcing your shoulders downward. No one needs to be any the wiser. Try it in front of a mirror at home, and see for yourself. Get into the habit. Do this tensioning procedure several times each day. It's a good exercise even if you don't have excess adrenaline to burn up. Try it now.

Another thing you can do to dispel nervous tension is breathe deeply, slowly, easily and rhythmically. It is also important to develop habits of good posture. Try not to slouch. Instead, maintain BALANCE in your posture. Sit with a straight back while attending to important matters. Observe your own posture frequently. A balanced, erect posture conserves energy.

Nervous tension, nervous agitation and fear are all infectious. You've probably noticed how agitated—even panicky—people are on Monday mornings and at other important times of the week. Have you noticed how infectious this agitation is? Even the most thick-skinned of us can be affected. The important thing is to be aware of its infectiousness. Just because everyone around you is agitated, it doesn't mean that you need to be. This awareness alone is often enough to break the spell. Don't be shy about being calm and relaxed when everyone else isn't. Your superior self-control will influence and impress them. You can calm down an entire crowd of people, just by becoming truly calm yourself. If you are unable to calm yourself down using the above observations, here's a technique you can use: Concentrate on breathing regularly. Breathe in slowly to the count of four and breathe out for a count of four. Keep your lungs empty for another count of four before repeating the steps. If you are walking, do this in time with your footsteps.

Help your body eliminate toxins

Toxins within the blood sap our vitality. Toxins get into the body via the air we breathe and the food we eat. Most of it however, is created by our own bodies. Our bodies are made up of billions of living cells. Each one, like all living things, takes in nutrients and excretes waste matter. The lymph fluid which surrounds all of our bodily tissue cells carries this waste matter away to the lymph nodes where it is neutralized and destroyed. The lymph system is like a sewage system. It is vital to our health, wellbeing and vitality. If it stopped working altogether, we'd be poisoned to death within twenty-four hours. Whereas the blood's circulatory system has a pump (the heart), the lymph system has none. It relies on muscular movement to keep the fluids moving. Even when we are fast asleep, the flow is maintained by the muscular action of our breathing, and our instinctive need to turn over occasionally.

Deep breathing relaxes you. It also makes the lymph system remove toxins up to fifteen times faster. It also provides the body's cells with more oxygen. Body cells become unhealthy without adequate oxygen—even malignant.

People who exercise frequently are statistically less likely to get cancer than people who don't. Aerobic exercise is the kind of exercise we need. Aerobics literally means 'exercising with air'—the kind of exercise that gets you out of breath. Try doing some aerobic exercise each day. You'll find your energy levels rise. Start off gently at first, and steadily increase it each day. A daily exercise routine is a very important secret of personal success. It will make you feel better, look better, perform better, and you'll live longer.

The other very important way of keeping your blood clean, thus improving your general health and energy levels is to drink plenty of pure water. Aim to drink around four pints of clean, pure water every day.

Eat plenty of fiber. This also is very important for detoxifying the system. The best kind is soluble fiber. Oats are rich in this.

Yoga & meditation

When people talk about yoga, they are often referring to the physical exercises. However, yoga is very much a mind and body enhancing system. Although the system was developed in India thousands of years ago, it could almost have been tailor made for the modern world. It is unsurpassed as a means of developing one's mental and physical well-being. I mention it here because it incorporates breathing exercises which, as already mentioned, clear the body of detrimental toxins.

Meditation is also a very effective way of overcoming emotional unrest. Unhealthy emotions can lie festering deep in our minds without our being aware of them. Resentment, guilt, jealousy, and the like can all sap our energies. Resolve those unhealthy emotions once and for all, either through meditation or by positive remedial action. Are you carrying with you a burden of bad feelings? If so, try to resolve them conclusively. If it's anger you're harboring, perhaps you should express your feelings to the persons involved, and then make peace with them. If it's your boss, perhaps you should compose a letter explaining your grievance and send it to him. Sometimes just writing a letter without even sending it is enough to resolve an inner conflict. If it is feelings of guilt that encumber you, can you perhaps make up for the wrong you've done, and then move on?

If you can't find a way to resolve these problems, at least find someone to whom you can talk about them. Offloading, verbally, is very therapeutic, especially when the listening ear is a sympathetic one. Psychiatrists and psychotherapists are aware of this. Their patients frequently cure themselves simply by expressing their inner problems to a receptive ear.

Practice being decisive

Finally, indecision can severely deplete your vitality. Sometimes it's better to risk making a wrong choice than to waste substantial time and energy. Wrong choices can often be rectified, but time lost through indecision cannot be replaced.

Sleep well

If you have stress hormones or accumulated tension in your system when you go to bed, you'll be unable to get a truly recuperative night's sleep. This means you will be putting your system under strain the following day. The following will help you sleep well:

- Do some fairly strenuous exercises during the evening (if your doctor approves).
- Avoid suspense filled, adrenaline-stimulating television programs late at night.

- Read something in bed, preferably something on success and motivation.
- Avoid caffeine. Alcohol is another stimulant that doesn't promote restful sleep.
- Taking a shower before bed helps you sleep well.

Some food combinations are difficult to digest and will prevent you from sleeping peacefully—for example, combinations of starch and protein. In the evening, avoid cheese, chocolate, wine, bacon, ham, sausage, potatoes and tomatoes. These foods all contain tyramine, which causes the body to produce norepinephrine, a brain stimulant.

Physical contact with someone close has a deeply calming effect. If you have no one close, or if you are living alone, do you have a pet? Affectionately stroking a cat, dog or other pet has a proven calming effect. It has been discovered that people who have a pet they are close to are less likely to contract heart disease.

Plan your next day the night before. Each night, write down the main things you must accomplish the following day, in order of their importance. Doing this will ease your mind during the night and when you wake up, because you won't be concerned about remembering your schedule.

More tips for reducing nervous tension

- **Keep your workplace and home tidy.** Working in an untidy place creates subtle uneasiness. A change is as good as a rest, so get the habit of tidying up as a form of break from your old routine.

- **Reduce your consumption of drinks containing caffeine.** The effect of caffeine is very similar to adrenaline. It puts a strain on your system.

- **Dwell on pleasant thoughts.** Just thinking about issues that worry you makes your body tense and therefore drains your energies. Focusing on the good things of life creates good emotions. Good emotions free up your energy.

- **Wash away positive ions.** If too many positively charged ions get into your body, they make you tired, tense and irritable. Ions are electrically charged particles about the size of an atom. A shower washes away those positive ions, making you feel uplifted and fresh.

- **Spend time occasionally, exclusively for unwinding.** During these periods, just do anything you feel like, and don't worry about wasting time. Take a holiday, or even just a weekend break. Give your brain a special treat and do something totally different for a change. Besides being mentally nourishing, a change is as good as a rest, as we've all been told. Find some different company for a while. Get amongst people who share your dreams and ambitions, if possible. Especially try to get among people who have succeeded in ways you want to succeed.

Get a head start on the world

If you are under pressure at work, consider starting work at least half an hour earlier each morning. By getting a head start, you won't feel so pressured to keep up with your competitors. And your boss will probably be impressed too.

Laugh!

Learn to evoke humor, even in anxious situations. A laugh has a powerful relaxing effect, and releases beneficial hormones into your system. Try keeping a pocket notebook of jokes that appeal to you, or perhaps you can try imagining the people around you as caricatures. One successful businessman says that during tense encounters, he imagines his opponents are dressed in nothing but underwear.

Love - the great panacea

There are many kinds of love, from romantic to maternal to fraternal to the love of life itself. Love makes life worth living. It generates vitality and gives us a feeling of gratitude and a reason for making an effort. So determine what it is that you really love, in the highest sense, and nourish it and appreciate it. Even a tiny spark of love can grow, spread, and magnify the glory of living, attracting the goodwill of people who are good for you. Love is a vibration that nourishes all. When you feel it, you emanate it. It attracts good fortune.

It is the view of the author that the best kind of love to cultivate is the all-encompassing type. This is the kind of love that, once developed, cannot fail you, because it is not dependent on one particular person for its fulfillment. It is closely related to the love of life itself, but perhaps goes even beyond that. You might think of it as 'higher love', because it is connected with spirit rather than our animal, egoistical or self-serving side.

It comes from within

How can you develop this most valuable of all qualities? You may already have it to some extent. It may have become buried, or perhaps you have never known it. That is not a problem because it is never too late to foster and nurture this special gift that is so universal in its benefits. To experience it, it has to exist within your own mind and the closely-connected heart. So first, we can think about it. We can contemplate it and all its appeal and merit. Once you have developed a clear idea of what it is, you can meditate on it with easier focus and immerse yourself in it more fully.

Resistance to meditating on Love

When you start to meditate on this all-encompassing love, you may find that opposing feelings try to gate-crash your party so to speak. Thoughts or feelings of cynicism, frustration, bitterness, irritation, or resentment may try to enter your mental space. Some wise people say that when this happens, it is best to acknowledge their existence but then guide your attention back onto your chosen path—the subject you have chosen to focus on.

The more you progress with this, the more you will notice your life and wellbeing improving in countless ways.

RECOMMENDED ACTION STEPS

1) Every night at bedtime, write down the six most important things that need doing, the following day. Write it in a pocket notebook or on a postcard that you can keep with you. You will sleep better and start the next day more relaxed. It's a powerful habit to adopt.

2) Make a note of the kind of projects that fire you up with energy and enthusiasm. Resolve to do more of them.

3) Start your own Laugh Book. Start recording all the jokes that tickle you. Keep it with you. Read it whenever things get too tense and serious.

4) Make a list of all the truly uplifting words you can think of and make a point of using them in your inner and outer dialogue at every opportunity.

5) Meditate regularly on all-encompassing love. The more you can do this with full attention, the more you will understand and appreciate its merits. Through full focus and overcoming the tendency of the unruly attention to wander, the more fully you can immerse your consciousness in it, and realize its full and wonderful benefits.

❖ *It is absurd to divide people into good and bad. People are either charming or tedious.—Oscar Wilde*

26
CHARM & CHARISMA
SECRETS OF PERSONAL MAGNETISM

❖ *Charm is… a way of getting the answer 'yes' without having asked any clear question.* —Albert Camus

Charm and charisma are qualities that everyone can develop. They are the oils that lubricate our axles on the rails to success and achievement. This chapter reveals the secrets of developing these qualities.

You have probably noticed that when you feel happy and optimistic, you attract favorable reactions from other people. Provided they are not in an overwhelmingly negative state (say, due to some recent misfortune), they light up when they see you. They immediately pick up on those positive vibrations. There is every advantage in maintaining this positive aura. It is the way to attract favorable events that can propel us to success. It can make you a wealth-magnet if wealth is what you seek.

Charm

One of the key secrets of personal charm seems to be in taking a genuine interest in other people and making them feel important and good about themselves. The need to feel important is one of the foremost human desires, so if you can help them satisfy that desire, you will charm them for sure.

❖ *The deepest craving of human nature is the need to feel valued and valuable. The secret of charm is therefore simple: make others feel important.*
   ---Brian Tracy & Ron Arden

Charisma

And what is charisma? It is the aura we have about us; the positive vibrations we emanate, through our optimism, goodwill, hope, confidence and leadership qualities.

❖ *Charisma is the result of effective leadership, not the other way around.—Warren Bennis and Burt Nanus*

Feel good about others

Life feels best when we feel goodwill for the people we live and work with, and the people we are surrounded by when we are out and about. If you have a natural and habitual outlook of unwavering goodwill for people then good for you! If not, then please try the following technique:

Just before you leave home to go out, take a few minutes to sit and release all traces of ill-will, antagonism and cynicism towards people in general and the world at large. Take a moment to consider that each individual has a unique set of difficulties and disadvantages that you cannot know about. Therefore you cannot fairly judge them for their attitudes and behaviors. To do so would be an act of substandard intelligence and insight. Reflect also on how easy it is to misjudge people and misinterpret their behavior or mannerisms. Consider also that as human beings, we are connected, and are ultimately close relatives with many shared difficulties – the difficulties that are inextricably part of being human on this planet of ours. Before you conclude, imagine yourself projecting goodwill in all four directions. Then release these thoughts into the universe, say "And so it is" and then leave home and enjoy your outing.

Physical wellbeing and good posture

Good posture is a highly beneficial habit to maintain. One of the main qualities of good posture is energy-efficiency and another is BALANCE. If the body is well balanced in its posture, it uses up far less energy. As a simple illustration, pick up a broom, garden rake or something similar; grasp the end of its handle and hold it upright. Notice how easy this is when the broom is perfectly upright. Now try to hold it so that it leans over a little. Notice how much more energy and concentration it takes to maintain this. The same effect applies if you don't maintain an upright, balanced posture.

Unfortunately, our muscles tend to assume the positions they are usually kept in. For example, if you spend nearly all day sitting at a desk, it becomes more difficult for the muscles to assume a good posture when standing up. The answer to this is physical exercise—the kind that both stretches muscles in positions they don't normally assume, and at the same time strengthens them. Apart from the excellent effect on posture, little needs to be said about the importance of exercise on the body in general.

A habitual daily exercise routine is extremely important for everyone. If you're in the habit of not exercising, it may take a little willpower to change this. However, it's easy if you follow this rule: Go gently at first, but don't miss a session unless you really have to. After a few days of keeping up your exercise routine, you will start to notice the improvement in your posture, stamina, and the way you feel. It then becomes more fun. Ideally, your daily exercise routine should include each of the following elements:

- Aerobic exercises that make your heartbeat and breathing rate increase: jogging, running on the spot, exercise biking and skipping, for example.
- Calisthenics, i.e. anything that strengthens your muscles: push-ups, sit-ups, weights, etc.
- Stretching. Yoga style exercises are the obvious example. It's a good idea to vary your exercises constantly, so that all your muscles can benefit.

Mental posture

Apart from bodily posture, mental posture is very important. Being in good physical shape by following the above tips will do much to improve your mental posture, but we can develop good mental posture independently to some extent. Good mental posture creates charisma too, and is just as important as physical posture. What do we mean by good mental posture? Just as we need to keep the body upright and balanced to avoid wasting energy, we need to keep our minds 'upright' too, to avoid wasting mental or emotional energy. Keep the mind upright by keeping the good things of life constantly in mind. Think continuously about all the things to be thankful for. Reflect habitually on love, goodwill, courage, truth, compassion, and success. To this end, take time every day to read something spiritually uplifting. Do this instead of watching frivolous TV programs or reading empty newspapers.

Movement

We send out non-verbal signals constantly, through the way we move. The way we move also affects how much energy we use up. It also affects our inner wellbeing. Good, efficient and graceful movement is as relaxed as possible, as smooth and non-jerky as possible, and as gentle as possible. Next time you are walking around, indoors or out, observe the way you are moving. Can you improve it at all? Poor styles of movement are infectious. If you go out on a Monday morning, you may notice that people are rushing around in semi-panic. On such occasions you must avoid becoming infected by the trend, and double your efforts to stay cool. You'll not only be doing yourself a favor, but the people around you too. Your unflustered movements will do much to break the vicious circle of mass panic. Again, Yoga is one of the best kinds of training for improving the way we carries ourselves. Tai Chi is also excellent in this respect. Any form of active sport is also excellent for those with the necessary enthusiasm to sustain and enjoy it.

Dress well

Artists and musicians, and to some extent writers, enjoy a certain amount of what we might call 'artistic license' when it comes to dress. If you fraternize with the more formal professions and social echelons you will find it pays dividends to dress well. In that case, dress well, but don't overdo it. There is a fine line between dressing that little bit better than average and going over the top. It pays to pay careful attention to what successful people typically wear when carrying out activities such as the one you are preparing for. When choosing your clothing, apart from needing to dress appropriately for the occasion, it is important to feel good about yourself. Pay attention both to style and color. Pick the exact color of the clothes you wear on the eve of the occasion itself. That way you can pick colors that will have just the right effect on your mood, without being unsuitable for the occasion. Obviously, you won't want to wear a multicolored suit to a funeral, but small details such as a man's tie can give that valuable opportunity for self-expression. Men: for important events, if you can afford it, wear a brand new shirt and tie that you have selected specially. Make sure the collar size is slightly loose. It doesn't help your cool image to have a face like a beetroot because you are being throttled by your own collar! Never buy the cheapest shirts you can find. Pay a bit more, and get one that feels good to wear, and doesn't let your Jack Daniels T-shirt show through! Pure cotton is considered more tasteful nowadays. Shirts that take cuff links are not so easy to find, but gold cuff links are a distinctive touch.

Gold is considered the magical metal. It is believed by some to attract money. If you want to become prosperous, wear gold. If you can't afford solid gold yet, get sneaky and wear gold plate! Gold can have an intimidating effect, so don't overdo it. A gold watch with a gold strap is a suitable accessory if you want to blend in with the rich and famous. A beautifully designed gold plated version can be bought for a few dollars, yet it still creates the right effect. Just hope that no-one asks for a close inspection! Make sure it is genuine gold or genuine gold plate. Other gold-colored metals won't do. It has been noted that usually, the more successful a person is, the simpler will be the design of his watch. Truly successful people seem unconcerned with having a watch that will tell the date, the time in every world city, play tunes, double as a calculator or a mini computer game. They usually go to the other extreme, and wear ones with no bells and whistles, but just tasteful design.

Shoes are another indicator of power and status. Out of all his clothing, the poor man who wants to look smart will give the lowest priority to his shoes, when cleaning up his image. Heels in particular should be checked for telltale wear and tear. The successful man doesn't usually display worn heels or tired shoes when he's dressed up. The poor, unsuccessful man usually does. This applies to women as well. So wear good quality shoes that are fairly new. Make sure they fit perfectly. Ill-fitting ones will work against you; perfectly fitting shoes that you feel just right in, are a powerful force in making you feel confident.

Be relaxed and cheerful

Easier said than done sometimes, perhaps, but we can cure ourselves of bad moods, and poor spirits. It usually takes a little self-discipline, but the remedies are within everyone's reach. Physical exercise, yoga, relaxation and meditation all have the effect of making you more relaxed, optimistic and cheerful—whatever your age. Keep in touch with people who make you happy. Real charisma comes from what's inside your head and in your heart, rather than what you're dressed in. So above all else, maintain a good attitude and a positive outlook, and keep your goals burning brightly!

Get known for what you have to offer!

One of the most effective ways to enjoy personal magnetism is to have some gift, skill or ability that people want to benefit from. Then see to it that these skills are known about in your community. The more your skill is widely in demand, the better. If you can help someone by applying this skill and then other people hear about it and want the same benefit for themselves you can soon reach something akin to celebrity status and your life and career will bring you full satisfaction.

Develop and deploy your winning smile.

A smile creates a positive impression and uplifts the general mood prevalent in your surroundings. Maintaining a slight smile when in the company of people will make all the difference. Display a broader one when interacting positively with people. Start training yourself today. Smile with your voice when you talk on the phone; the person at the other end of the line will detect it and be positively influenced by it. If you're self-conscious about your smile, develop one that you're proud of. Work on it in the mirror. Even a slight smile is far better than no smile. It conveys higher intelligence! If you face the world with a typical glum or grim expression, you'll only attract negative experiences and reactions. Get the habit of smiling. Try to ensure you always have a smile on your face, to one extent or another. This is a powerfully effective habit.

Practice eye-contact when interacting

A good degree of eye contact when interacting with people has great benefits. It shows that you are paying attention. It shows that you care about what the other person feels and thinks. It suggests honesty. Be careful not to overdo it with someone who displays unease. However use it with discretion. Different cultures have different norms of civility. In some cultures, eye contact with the opposite sex is considered flirtatious. In many Asian, African and Latin American cultures, sustained eye contact can be taken as an affront or a challenge of authority. Among natives of most western countries however, it is generally a positive thing that usually promotes trust and mutual respect.

Personal hygiene

This chapter would be incomplete without this! Place high importance on personal cleanliness. You'll create negative reactions if you're not physically clean and hygienic. Even slight amounts of stale body odor can adversely affect people's reaction to you. So shower or bathe daily and always have fresh breath and clean teeth. Besides cleaning your teeth after breakfast, have a tube of toothpaste and a toothbrush at work or in your car, and use it during the day; immediately after lunch is a good time. Such details make you feel better about yourself and make others feel better about you. When people aren't distracted by someone's body odor, grimy fingernails or oily facial skin, communication will flow more freely, and their reaction to you will be more positive.

The amazing benefits of a warm shower!

Taking a warm shower is therapeutic and energizing, and benefits you instantly and powerfully in more ways than just getting you clean:

- Tension-creating positive ions get washed down the drain.
- It balances out the temperature differences of various areas of your body, improving circulation of blood and electrochemical energy.
- It relaxes you, freeing up potential energy for easier, more efficient action.
- The act of towel-drying yourself is good exercise, and a good form of massage. Do it vigorously; it exercises muscles that don't normally get a workout.

RECOMMENDED ACTION STEPS

1) If you tend to harbor ill-will and cynicism towards people, spend a few minutes before leaving home, releasing all ill-will and project good will in all four directions. Consider how all individuals are related as fellow human beings. Consider that each person out there has a unique set of problems and disadvantages that we cannot possibly know about, so we cannot reasonably judge them by their behavior. Consider how easy it is to misinterpret actions and mannerisms.

2) Get the habit of looking presentable before you go out, even if it is merely a trip to the local supermarket.

3) Take up some form of regular physical discipline such as calisthenics, yoga, running or training at your local gym.

4) Develop some skill (if you don't already have one) that has the potential to benefit people in your community. Then see to it that your skill is known about.

5) Get the habit of smiling to people, and maintaining a good degree of eye contact while in conversation.

6) Maintain a good degree of eye contact during interactions with Anglo-Americans and Europeans. Remember: people of the opposite sex may consider it flirtatious.

7) Develop the habit of making an effort to value everyone you meet, make them feel good about themselves. Make them feel important. It's the way to be well-liked and popular and that can only be good! Above all: maintain a positive mental attitude, which should come naturally while you follow the methods outlined in this book!

❖ *The most important thing in communication is hearing what isn't said.*—Peter F. Drucker

27
NON-VERBAL COMMUNICATION
PAY ATTENTION TO IT!

❖ *What you do speaks so loud that I cannot hear what you say.* —Ralph Waldo Emerson

Communication is everything. Without it we are lost. The better we can communicate, the more effectively we can live and progress. Having a good command of English is of course highly advantageous. But as Mae West famously said: "I speak two languages, Body and English". Psycholinguists now hold that as much as 80% of everything we communicate is expressed through body language! Therefore it naturally helps to be skilled at understanding and using *that* language...

Non-verbal communication refers to the body-language messages we are constantly sending to the people around us. We've all heard of it, but few are consciously aware of it—or the importance of it—or the astounding amount of it that goes on. You can augment your personal power by your understanding and awareness of it.

Professor A. Meharbian of the University of California researched the subject and concluded that only about seven per cent of the interpersonal communication that takes place is verbal and explicit. About thirty-eight per cent is implicit and gets across via other means; for example, so-called paralanguage. That is, the inflections, tone and volume of the voice. The other fifty-five per cent is conveyed by body language. Much of this non-verbal communication takes place on a subconscious level. Once we are aware of this, we can benefit in many ways:

- We can understand better what people are thinking and feeling.
- We can gain control of our own body language to project the right messages.
- We will find it easier to make friends and foster good relationships.

These benefits are useful to everyone, especially those whose work involves selling or negotiating. And let's face it: everyone is involved in selling and negotiating. We all need to 'sell' ourselves and most human interactions involve some form of negotiation.

An important tactic for personal success is to develop the habit of making a favorable impression—especially during the all-important first two minutes of any new encounter. It has been shown that most people pass judgment on a new acquaintance within the first two minutes of the first encounter, and it is their body language, more than the words spoken, that forms the basis of this judgment. After this critical two minutes, impressions that corroborate this already formed opinion are given credence while others are treated with relative skepticism. Therefore, be sure to make the best possible impression during the first two minutes of every important new encounter.

Interpret body language cautiously

When we learn about body language, it is important to view the subject in the right perspective. Body language signals are often misinterpreted. Therefore resist the inclination to jump to conclusions with the body language signals you see. For example: a person who rubs his earlobe may be wishing to glean more information from you. On the other hand, he may just have an itchy ear. When someone makes a body language gesture in reaction to something that is being said or done, then this is more reliable. Remember also that people from different cultures have very different body language mannerisms. A body language signal to a westerner may mean something totally different if carried out by someone from the Far East. Customs can even vary from one part of a country to another.

You can greatly accelerate your understanding of body language by studying people. Do this whenever you can observe people without being able to hear what they are saying—for example, when you are in a restaurant, watching people outside.

Body language is important because it is difficult to fake. Some people have an uncanny knack of detecting lies just by understanding body language.

The eyes

People give out a large amount of their silent speech signals with their eyes. What's more, the language of the eyes is fairly reliable, hard to cover up and hard to fake. If you learn to understand the language of the eyes, you can read a person's unspoken thoughts and feelings. Eyes 'speak' through the pupils, the eyelids, eye-movements and the eyebrows.

The pupils

How can we tell what a person really feels about us? If we listen only to the voice and the words spoken, we are in danger of being misled. People can easily mislead with words, and it is all too easy to control the tone of voice. The eyes however—as we've all heard—are considered the windows of the soul.

We all know that the pupil of the eye gets bigger when the light gets low, but there is something else which affects pupil size: our emotions. When we see something we really like or desire, our pupils will enlarge, almost instantly. So look out for this tell-tale signal. Professional gamblers who know about this wear dark glasses, so as not to give away their reaction to the hand they have been dealt.

The eyelids

How can we tell if someone is interested in what we are saying or doing? Observe the position of the eyelids. When a person is truly interested, their upper eyelids will open higher. If they open so much that the whites of the eyes above the eyelids show, you can be sure they are very interested. If, on the other hand, the eyelids are lowered, so they cover part of the pupil, you can suspect they may be bored. Ultimately, of course, the eyelids will close completely, and the person is so bored that he has fallen asleep!

The frequency of eye blinking is another important signal. First, you need to know the subject's natural blink rate. This can vary from about fifteen blinks per minute to about once every second. Once you know this, you can notice if their blink rate changes suddenly in reaction to something being said. When their blink rate changes suddenly, it usually means they are intensely interested, or becoming tense or emotionally affected.

Eye movements

We can tell a great deal about a person by the way the eyes move. If a person is trying to conceal something, he or she may try to avoid looking us in the eye. This is probably due to an unconscious knowledge that their eyes might give the game away.

However, when someone does look us in the eye, we can tell a lot about them by the direction their eyes move when they look away. If a person is bored with you or what you are saying, he may break eye contact by looking upwards. Shifty eyes often indicate that the person is on the defensive, on the lookout for someone who might discover his secret, or he may be 'looking' for ideas—ways out—out of his current predicament.

The eyebrows

We all know what it means when someone raises an eyebrow at something; it means that someone suspects that the thing in question raises suspicion of being out of order, dishonest, inappropriate, etc.

Posture

The general posture of a person gives a very reliable indication of his attitude.

When a person is slouching, either while walking, sitting or standing, it suggests something negative in his attitude. When you are talking to someone and they cross their legs or arms, it often indicates they have reservations or are feeling defensive about what you are saying. Conversely, when they loosen up their posture, it usually indicates greater acceptance. If they sit up and lean towards you slightly, this usually indicates that they are becoming more interested. If they sit back, put their feet up on the table and clasp their hands behind their heads, they are usually in a position of power—within the immediate environment, at least.

Tell-tale actions

If they take off their glasses and start cleaning the lenses with a handkerchief, it could indicate a desire to have things made clearer. If they keep positioning things neatly on the table—papers, cutlery or whatever, it can mean they intend to keep control of the conversation and keep it efficient and orderly. If they start playing with an object, observe how they are playing with it. This can tell you much about their mental approach to the discussion. Are they stroking it, smoothing it, stabbing it, pushing it, moving it around, balancing it, or dividing it into two piles?

Bear in mind that they may be subconsciously using these actions as a form of communication. The orderly dividing up of crumbs may be a subtle way of inspiring you to help keep the dialogue well organized.

Power signals

Many non-verbal signals can give clues about a person's level of power. Supposing you were given a new job, and you were thrust into the midst of the staff and employees without having been introduced to any of them. It's important that you convey the right level of subservience to each person as appropriate. If you don't, you may well be about to get many important relationships off on the wrong footing. This is not so easy when it's one of those companies where everyone dresses the same.

How can you tell which ones you should approach with a dominant attitude and which ones you should react to with a subservient air? Here are some clues: How fast are they moving about? Usually, the more they are hurrying, the more frightened they are. The man at the top (or the one with the most power) usually moves at a more leisurely pace. He gets others to do the rushing around. Be aware though, that the people with the most power are not always the ones with the highest rank. If the washroom cleaner is doing a job that is vital to the well-being of the company, and there's no one else willing to do it, then he/she may have considerable power! He may not, of course, realize it, but treat him with respect, just in case; likewise, the secretary who may know some the chairman's guilty secrets.

Apart from body language, there are other forms of non-verbal communication: the clothes people wear, the style of their personal transport and the accessories they carry. Those with the highest status often travel in chauffeur-driven cars, and never carry briefcases or have pens projecting from their top pockets. They often display telltale gestures such as the princely 'fingers up the shirt cuff fiddle' favored by Prince Charles. (I still don't know what that one is all about; making sure the Derringer or the secret microphone is correctly positioned, perhaps!) There's also the 'Napoleonic hand-inside-lapel' pose favored by Herman Goring and Napoleonic wannabes. Such mannerisms can be the mark of someone with genuine high status. However, many people in official positions use them slyly to garner respect, so don't regard them as an infallible indication of status!

Use it consciously (S.O.F.T.E.N.)

Use non-verbal communication to SOFTEN the hard-line position of others:

S: Smile
O: Open Posture
F: Forward Lean
T: Touch
E: Eye Contact
N: Nod

❖ *When the eyes say one thing, and the tongue another, a practiced man relies on the language of the first.*
—*Ralph Waldo Emerson*

RECOMMENDED ACTION STEP

Next time you are in town, treat yourself to a cup of coffee. Sit near a window where you can observe the people outside but not hear them. Start honing your body language interpretation skills! Notice what people are communicating, intentionally or otherwise, in nonverbal ways.

❖ *Networking is about making meaningful, lasting connections that lead to one-to-one relationships.—Les Garnas*

28
A NETWORK OF SUPPORTERS
THE NON-ISLAND APPROACH

❖ *Every great athlete, artist and aspiring being has a great team to help them flourish and succeed - personally and professionally. Even the so-called 'solo star' has a strong supporting cast helping them shine, thrive and take flight.*
—Rasheed Ogunlaru

In this chapter we explore one of the key strategies of those people who mysteriously achieve inordinately rapid success in major endeavors: the policy of intelligent, selective networking—as opposed to attempting to succeed as a living, breathing island!

The old saying goes: "No man is an island." Never was this truer than in the field of worldly success and achievement. A person with a network of backers, allies, or helpers is many times more effective than the person who tries to go it alone. The super-achievers of the world usually know this instinctively, and owe their rise to personal success to the considerable help they have had along the way from friends, contacts, relatives and associates. Their backers are people with whom they have a special kind of relationship: generally the easy-going kind, typical of friends and relatives. Each member of this network will specialize in some subject that is of key importance, or perform a specific role in the success-seeker's rise to success. Such a network of supporters will save you a fortune in time and expense.

The main point of the supporting network is that it provides the success-seeker with a rich source of inside knowledge, advice, and support, often free of charge, once the relationship has developed successfully and trust has been built. Getting the services of professionals can be expensive. Yet most professionals will give free advice to their friends and relatives. If the members of your support network know about you and your interests, their advice will tend to be more useful than professional advice coming from a complete stranger. And their help will often be performed with more involvement. That's the way it is among friends and relatives. Money rarely changes hands. More usually, what changes hands is another kind of currency: information, support, friendship, and personal favors. It may cost your network supporter nothing to swing a door, or say a word in someone's ear, or pull a string in your favor, yet such small pieces of help can sometimes result in vast fortunes being made, or expensive disasters being averted.

How to develop your network

It is a good idea to make a list of the 20 to 50 people who you would most like to establish a mutually beneficial relationship with in the coming year, and then plan how best to approach each of these key people in the first place. Thanks to the Internet, the geographical limits are now virtually non-existent.

If you want to approach high-flying influencers who are in exceptionally good positions to help your career, it is really necessary to have something to offer them, to make it worth their while to respond to your contact. Only you know what you have to offer, so I cannot provide any specific advice in this respect. If you can identify some way you can benefit them, and they do not initially respond, don't give up. Send a follow-up message after a week or two. Be brief; busy people are unlikely to want to read a long email or letter from someone they don't know unless what you have to offer them is genuinely irresistible. Point out any commonalities you share with the individual, to establish some kind of rapport.

Never push them too far. If they think you're 'using' them excessively, or just being a pest, they'll soon make themselves unavailable. So, be sensitive at all times. Try to maintain a sense of humor, and a relaxed, positive, and cheerful attitude. Don't burden them with your problems. In fact, it's best if they don't even get to know you have any. Don't try to be too chummy with your proposed supporters if you haven't known them long. Ultimately, you want them to be your friend, but don't rush this process.

A very basic network

There follows a very basic list of typical supporters that might form a basic network for practically anyone. The ones we've chosen are universally useful, so you will probably want to add these to a list of others that are more pertinent to your own situation. You may find you already have some of these people among your existing circle of friends and relatives.

The encouraging supporter

This person helps you believe in your new ideas and projects. He or she reminds you of your strengths and talents, and helps you develop a positive self-image.

The constructive critic

Bounce your new ideas off this person, who should have a very practical and objective thinking style. He or she will detect and draw your attention to any weaknesses in your plans.

The financier

It's good to have someone who can lend you money when needed. Personal contacts—friends and relatives especially—can be more flexible and sympathetic than banks.

The ideas person

The ideas person will be a good lateral thinker, who can suggest new ideas that can get you past any mental blocks that hinder your progress. This person loves to put his creative imagination to work, so he's unlikely to demand remuneration.

The problem solver

The problem solver is another kind of ideas person, but one with a propensity for resolving dilemmas. He or she will often be an understanding type, who is glad to help out someone with a problem.

The IT wizard

If you use, or are ever likely to use, a computer, this fellow is a must. Computers and the software that they use are extremely advanced pieces of technology. No matter how much you are able to learn about them yourself, there invariably comes a day when something baffles you, or goes wrong. Advice can be expensive. A visit by a service engineer can be even more expensive. What's more, the professional advisor often has a vested interest in getting you to pay for a visiting engineer, or a new component. Your friendly neighborhood geek, on the other hand, is often only too glad to impress you with his knowledge, and can more often than not solve your problem in a couple of minutes over the telephone. He will also save you a fortune when it comes to choosing new equipment. Buying new equipment is a minefield, and there are only two ways around it: Either spend hours reading comparative test results in the computer press, or... ask your friendly computer buff.

The legal expert

Lawyers are notoriously expensive, and sometimes of questionable value. A trip to a reference library can be time consuming and tedious. A five minute chat with your legal friend on the other hand is sweet, simple and cheap. Look for one who specializes in the area of law that's most important to you.

The local government contact

Try to get one as high up the local government hierarchy as possible—someone with as much power and influence as possible, and someone who knows as much as possible about the ins and outs of the various local government departments. Such a contact can be useful in many problems that involve local government. These can include: getting planning permission, sorting out issues with local taxation, dealing with nuisance neighbors and settling disagreements with local services, businesses and utility providers. Local government can often be a big stumbling block in the path of personal progress, so be sure to develop a friendly contact there.

The police contact

The difference between a big problem with the police and no problem at all can be due to something as trivial as which side of the bed a particular police officer got out of the morning in question. If you fall foul of a prejudiced or vindictive police officer, be sure to make a note of his number, which should be displayed on his uniform. Failing that, get his name. This action alone will usually be enough to make him more careful about his behavior. However, if you still end up being unfairly treated, you can sometimes be in a stronger position if you have a contact in the police force—ideally someone with some power and influence. Often, a few words with the right colleague from this person can get you off the hook. Or, if your rights have been violated, it can even result in justice being done (but don't count on it). If you are on chatting terms with this contact, you can get a great deal of valuable insight into which laws you need to observe, and which ones you can safely ignore. Some laws are accepted as inappropriate to the current day and age, and are not enforced. You can get all kinds of useful information about your neighborhood from a friendly police person.

Progress is hard when relegated to an island...

Don't be afraid to ask for help

Many people are reluctant to ask for help from a neighbor, friend or contact. They dread feeling indebted to anyone. But this is usually a foolish position to adopt. Research has shown that people actually tend to like people they have done favors for. That is, assuming that the favor was done in good will. Most people enjoy doing people favors, provided they don't feel they are being taken advantage of.

So do not be reluctant to ask favors. Asking a favor can also be a great way of breaking the ice and getting to know someone. Many harmonious neighborhood friendships have begun with one neighbor asking a favor of another. In fact, such harmonious relationships are more likely to result from one neighbor asking a favor of the other than from one neighbor attempting to do a favor for another without having been asked! This suggests most people feel more comfortable when someone is indebted to them than vice versa.

Of course, it is a wise person who fully respects and honors the other's right to refuse the favor, without holding any resentment or passing judgment upon them. You are less likely to be refused if you approach the other person with a degree of humility, free of any assumption that they will, or ought to, oblige.

❖ *The size of your network doesn't matter - it is the quality of your network that counts.* —Unknown

❖ *Everyone should build their network before they need it.* —Dave Delaney

RECOMMENDED ACTION STEPS

1) In your A-Log, start compiling a list of the members of your supportive network. It reminds you who you can go to for the different kinds of help you need in your rise to success and fulfillment.
2) Make a positive effort to find the supporters you need. When you find a new supporter, add the name to your list.
3) If you are in business for yourself, make a list of the 20 to 50 key movers and shakers you would most like to develop a friendship with in the coming year, and then plan your approach carefully, making sure you have something genuinely useful to offer them, to make it worth their while to interact with you.

29
30+ POWER HABITS
TO OPTIMIZE YOUR FUTURE

❖ *Men's natures are alike; it is their habits that separate them.* —Confucius

Our habits have a profound effect on our destiny, our fortune and our quality of life. There are bad habits. There are good habits. Then there are *Power Habits*—the habits that bring tremendous benefits with minimal effort. This chapter suggests some particularly formidable habits that every success-oriented person can adopt, to fabulous effect.

❖ *Thoughts lead on to purposes; purposes go forth in action; actions form habits; habits decide character; and character fixes our destiny.* —Tryon Edwards

Adopting these power habits can transform your life and your future. To reap their phenomenal rewards, it is best to repeat these practices until they become habitual. Doing so is not a chore though, because they are all immediately rewarding, bringing rapid benefits.

POWER HABIT 1
Be aware of and question your self-talk.

Become aware of what you are telling yourself about everything you experience throughout each day. Once you become aware of that self-talk, you can then question it! Much of it is programming that you adopted at a young age. Much of it is no longer useful or helpful—if indeed it ever was. Displace any negative self-talk with positive statements and affirmations of your own conscious choosing. Frame everything in positive terms. You are what you think, so make sure that all your inner monologue is positive. Positive thinking is one of the most valuable habits you can adopt. That is why we have made this Power Habit No.1.

POWER HABIT 2
Formulate your personal code of living.

In your A-Log, write out your personal code of living. This may not be easy to complete at first, but I want you to come back to this task every day at bedtime, and amend, develop, expand and adjust it as you see fit. This habit will have tremendous effects on your personal development and potential for fulfillment. Your code of living is fundamental. It is made up of the values you hold most dear, that govern the way you wish to live in years to come.

POWER HABIT 3
Every day, spend time behaving like the person you want to become.

In your A-Log, you described the person you would like to become. Be sure to review this description regularly. Now spend some time every day, behaving like this person. Don't let yourself off the hook—make this a habit. As time passes, spend more time each day behaving like this person, until eventually, you are behaving like this person 24/7. That's when you will genuinely adopt the characteristics you desire, and the new you will have become established.

POWER HABIT 4
Write down the goals that are most important to you.

In your A-Log, write down some goals that you can work towards. Choose them carefully. Make sure they are goals that you would really like to achieve—the goals you consider most desirable in your life. Do not be afraid to aim high! This program will give you the power to achieve much more than you may have thought possible. Forget everything you (or anyone else) has told you about what you are not capable of. Decide what would be a realistic but optimistic time frame by which you will aim to achieve each major goal. Write it down. Write down the actual completion date that you will aim for.

POWER HABIT 5
Break down your major goals into smaller interim steps.

Once you have settled on one or more major goals that you are ready to commit to, in your A-Log, break each of them down into a number of interim steps that would lead you to the achievement of the main goal. By doing this with care, seemingly impossible goals can become achievable. Amend as necessary when you review your A-Log each night at bedtime.

POWER HABIT 6
Every night, review your goals, visualize the successful outcome - and plan the steps you'll take to get there!

As you lie in bed, visualize the goal that is most important to you, and visualize the successful outcome of the achievement of your goals in as much detail as possible. Then mentally plan the steps you can take to achieve it. Planning and imagining these steps is just as important as imagining your enjoyment of the achieved goal. This power habit is the opposite of what losers do—they focus excessively on the outcomes they DON'T want to happen!

POWER HABIT 7
Take a step towards a major goal every day.

Take at least one step towards each of your main goals every day—without fail! Sometimes you will only be able to take a small step, but make sure you take it, every single day you live. Every great journey begins with a single step, and every great achievement is simply a succession of smaller, easier achievements. "Inch by inch, it's a cinch. By the yard, it's hard!" This is one of the most valuable habits you can ever adopt!

POWER HABIT 8
Take stock of your mental and material assets.

Try to list all of your assets. These will include material assets, intellectual assets, talents, abilities, helpful contacts, and all of the resources at your disposal. Add to this list as things occur to you. Develop the list when you review your A-Log, every night at bedtime. When you lie down to go to sleep, imagine how you can make use of these resources to help you achieve your goals.

POWER HABIT 9
Become goal-oriented.

Every day, each of us has to make hundreds of decisions and choices. I urge you to make these choices based on which one will best hasten the achievement of your goals. Consider every choice, from what you have for breakfast, to what mode of transport you use to get from A to B, how you spend your lunch break, what you watch on television, and who you talk with at a social or business event. Each time you are tempted to spend money, ask yourself: "Will this help me achieve my goals more quickly?"

POWER HABIT 10
Make a seven-day resolution - and stick to it at all costs!

This is an incredibly powerful technique. Choose some course of action or behavior that you can stick to for just seven days. Make it something that will move you closer to the achievement of your goals. Only choose a course of action that you can stick to WITHOUT FAIL. Then stick to it WITHOUT FAIL. Some big changes are daunting (giving up smoking for example). However, resolving to adhere to your chosen course of action for just seven days is a lot less daunting than sticking to it indefinitely. If you stick to your chosen course of action or behavior for the seven days, the affect on your morale and self-respect and confidence will be tremendous. Failing to adhere for seven days will, however, be seriously harmful to your self-respect and self-confidence, so, again, make sure you stick to your chosen course, *no matter what*.

POWER HABIT 11
Every night, write down the six most important tasks for the following day.

This stratagem is amazingly helpful. It makes you 100% more effective and stress-free! At bedtime, every night, you write down your six most important tasks for the following day, in order of their importance. Then forget about them and go to sleep. You will find that you sleep much better for having done this. Your subconscious mind knows it can now let go of all concerns about the next day, because you have written down the key actions you need to take. That sheet of paper will still be there when you wake up! Meanwhile, your subconscious mind will be digesting your task-list as you sleep, so that next day, you will find that things go much better than they otherwise might have done. You can refine your list of tasks by categorizing them as 'must do', 'should do', or 'could do'. A neat way to do this would be to prefix each item with 'M' (must do), 'S' (should do) or 'C' (could do). When tomorrow arrives, focus on getting the 'M' items done first. Then focus on the 'S' items, followed by the 'C' items.

POWER HABIT 12
When faced with any problem or challenge, think: "Which are the key factors?"

Bring your attention to bear on the main factors that form the core of each problem or challenge that you face. Don't fritter away your attention on the peripheral aspects of the problem, but cut to the chase. Before every important meeting, write down the six most important issues to cover. If you make a list of all the factors you can think of that pertain to the issue, you will easily be able to see which are the key points. Problems are often easily solved by concentrating on these alone!

POWER HABIT 13
Every day, write down six new things you are grateful for.

Studies in neuroscience have established that if you write down three things you are grateful for, and do this every day for at a three weeks, you effectively rewire your brain to be more optimistic. So let's make this another power habit to adopt. Keep it up for the next three weeks, and then you may decide to continue this effective technique for the rest of your life! Research indicates that even if you were to cease this habit after three weeks, you will still be experiencing the positive benefits six months later!

POWER HABIT 14
Tackle the most important tasks first.

Every day, tackle the most important tasks first! Do this, even if the most important items are the least appealing! Fit in the less important tasks afterwards if time permits. If you do not adopt this strategy in your daily life, you will find yourself tackling the most important tasks when you have insufficient time, and/or when you are already exhausted from having tackled the less important tasks first, instead of last. If you don't tackle the most important tasks first, you may never have time to accomplish them! Consider this: 20% of the tasks you accomplish produce 80% of the results. So do those 20% first, every day, while you have the most mental and physical energy.

POWER HABIT 15
Pursue a creative hobby.

A creative hobby makes you a more creative person. This, in turn, makes you a more positive person. The increased level of creativity that you'll develop will have powerful benefits in all areas of your life. Your increased level of creativity and your increasingly positive outlook will make you a people-magnet. Your social life will improve and so will your professional life. Find out if there are any groups in your area focusing on the hobby you have chosen and consider joining one. Meeting people who pursue the same hobby as you is a great way of making new friends - and everyone needs good friends!

POWER HABIT 16
Develop your network of supporters.
Keep a list of your supporting allies. Update it regularly, as you continuously strive to improve and develop your network. Most successful people rely on other people to help them become successful. No man is an island. Helpful contacts are potentially one of your most powerful resources.

POWER HABIT 17
Give good value in all your dealings.
Always give that little bit extra, even though it wasn't asked of you. More important perhaps, ALWAYS stick to your word. If you say you are going to do something, do it. People find it very irritating when someone doesn't stick to their undertaking. Every time you break your word in this way, you run a serious risk of destroying people's confidence in you. Always do what you agreed to do—and a bit more. This habit attracts success. It attracts goodwill. It attracts customers if you're in business. It is also good for your self-esteem.

POWER HABIT 18
Go all out on your present situation for one whole day.
Spend one whole day, working quickly and efficiently at doing all those minor jobs you've been putting off, but which need doing. Tie up all those loose ends. Do all those little and

not so little things that are constantly nagging you for attention. This special action can be likened to hacking out a clearing in the middle of a jungle or a forest. Once you have the clearing, you are free to get yourself organized and start building your super new future according to the goals you've already mapped out.

POWER HABIT 19
Look for the silver lining in every cloud.

Every cloud does have a silver lining, though it may not always seem obvious. One of the key skills of the world's most effective people is the adoption of this technique. At the very least, we can regard each setback as a valuable learning experience, but often it is much more. Whether we gain or lose from any situation is down to how and what we think about it. So think very carefully about every perceived 'problem' and learn to see how it, or some aspect of it, could actually be an advantage. After mastering this invaluable skill, you will never again need to feel disheartened in the face of perceived setbacks.

POWER HABIT 20
Break out of your routine.

One of the main reasons why most people are not successful in life is that their minds are imprisoned in the straitjacket of habitual thought patterns. Do everything in your power to break out of these limiting habits of thought. Every day, try something different. Drive to work by a different route—or ride a bicycle! Eat somewhere different. Buy yourself some differently styled clothes. Try some different form of entertainment. Do things you would never normally do—and with an open mind. Tear off the blinkers of habitual thinking and living. You can even put yourself in an instantly more open-minded state by crossing your legs in the opposite way to your habitual one. Try putting your watch on the other wrist. Even try writing with the other hand.

POWER HABIT 21
Develop and deploy your winning smile.

A smile is a passport to privilege. It creates a positive impression. Even when walking or driving, a slight smile will make all the difference. Start training yourself today. It may take some effort at first, as though tremendous forces are working against you, but force yourself to cut through all that, regardless. Smile also with your voice when you talk on the phone. If you're self-conscious about your smile, develop one that you're proud of. Work on it in the mirror. Even a slight smile works wonders. If you face the world with a typical glum or grim expression, you'll only attract negative experiences and reactions. Get into the habit of smiling. Try to ensure you always have a smile on your face, to one extent or another. This is a powerfully effective habit.

POWER HABIT 22
Be selective in what you watch, read and listen to.

Become aware of how much of your time you may be frittering away on empty television programs and newspapers and Internet sites that don't tell you anything useful or help you towards achieving your chosen goals. Switch your attention to activities that do.

95% of the contents of all newspapers and television programs are useless input that merely wastes your time, and fills your mind with negativity and depravity and stimulates counter-productive stress hormones. Most public media content and entertainment are designed to make money for someone else, and have no concern for your best interests. Resist the temptation to watch suspense-filled movies late at night when you need to be winding down and resting deeply. If you find yourself with time to kill, why not review your goals. Refine and revise your goals and affirmations. Read the biographies of successful people with qualities you'd like for yourself.

POWER HABIT 23
Improve your vocabulary.

To a large extent, one's success is governed by the quality of one's communication. Words are the raw material of communication, and the more of them we have at our disposal, the better we can communicate. So work on your vocabulary. There's little advantage in learning words that no-one understands, but do learn to use a greater number of the words people do understand. Every time you hear a familiar word that you don't fully know the meaning of, look it up in a dictionary. Make a point of using the new word a few times so that it doesn't get forgotten again. Write it down. Try to obtain a dictionary that gives you the derivation of words. It is sometimes enlightening to discover a word's origin.

Use more uplifting, energizing words in your internal and external dialogue. Every word you think and speak affects your whole being. So use uplifting words whenever you can - words like fantastic, amazing, brilliant, awesome, spectacular, phenomenal, sublime, ecstatic, divine, heavenly, fabulous, wonderful, etc.

POWER HABIT 24
Pay off your debts.

Set aside ten per cent or more of your income for this. Stick to it, sacrificing luxuries if necessary. You will hardly notice the difference, yet you'll be making positive steps towards success. Being free of debt will lift a great weight from you. The energy you were expending on worrying and extra work to pay interest can now be put to much more fruitful use. Sell off unneeded assets to pay off debts, if you have any. Beware of hanging on to assets that you don't really need, if you are in debt.

POWER HABIT 25
Eat wisely and exercise.

To get the most out of life you need energy and vitality. Therefore it's essential to eat a healthy diet. Cut down on sugars, refined starches and fats. Opt for decaffeinated tea or coffee. It is best to keep your alcohol intake very low. If you are overweight, get slim. Use the techniques in this program to attain this goal.

POWER HABIT 26
Mix with successful people.

Spend as little time and as little thought as possible on negative and pessimistic people. Instead, spend more time with the people who are successful in ways you want to be.

Their mental attitudes will rub off on you, and remember, attitude is more powerful than aptitude. This action-technique holds tremendous power to change your fortunes. If you are not in a position to mix with successful people, then at least read the biographies of people you admire.

POWER HABIT 27
Do favors for people at every opportunity.

Meet as many new people as you can by performing some small service to each one—with no wish to receive anything in return. You will find many opportunities to do this; pick up a coin for an elderly gent; help a mother up some steps with her pushchair; help someone with their heavy luggage; hold that elevator for someone; hold the door open for the lady with her arm full of shopping. Do unto others as you would have them do unto you. Word quickly spreads and the word will get around that you are a good person, but more importantly, it will boost your own self-esteem.

POWER HABIT 28
Ask and accept favors.

It's a remarkable thing—and contrary to what one might expect, but it has been discovered that people are more likely to think favorably of people they have done favors for, that of people who have done favors for them. So it would appear that in some cases, a more effective way to be popular is to accept favors rather than to grant them! This is not to say that you should not do people favors. Just don't be surprised if sometimes they don't seem as appreciative as you might expect.

POWER HABIT 29
Keep the word SUCCESS in mind.

Write the word SUCCESS on some small cards, and stick one on your mirror, and one on the dashboard of your car. Stick another in the place where you usually gaze when you lie down and relax. Remind yourself about success wherever you can. Reflecting on its meaning, even if only momentarily or subconsciously, will have a positive effect on your life. If you wish, you can be more specific, and use a word like WEALTH, if wealth is what success means to you.

POWER HABIT 30
Meditate daily.

Meditate first thing in the morning, and again, last thing at night. If this is impractical, then start with one session a day. This requires you to exercise self-discipline, but this is only one of the benefits! Every meditation session is extremely beneficial—even if you do not experience immediate benefits, they will still occur. It is not what you actually experience during meditation that is important; it's the degree of self-mastery that you gain. Done correctly, it will clear your mind of all the unhelpful mental clamor and re-establish calmness and mental focus that will multiply your effectiveness and your capacity to enjoy life. They say we are what we think, so if you are in any doubt about what to meditate upon, why not focus on the very best that life has to offer, such as the great panacea: all-encompassing, pure love.

POWER HABIT 31
Read and reflect on words of wisdom daily. Here is a selection for starters:

- *Life is not about finding yourself. Life is about creating yourself.* —Lolly Daskal

- *Nothing in the world is more common than unsuccessful people with talent.* —Anonymous

- *When a person becomes too busy to appreciate all the beautiful things in life, then that person is daily becoming poorer, not richer. To say that time is money devalues time. Get your enjoyment out of life; you deserve it. Money can be taken away from you, but what the heart has held can never be taken away.* —Ted Blake

- *The longer you work in the right direction, the closer you are to success.* —Napoleon Hill

- *I don't know the key to success, but the key to failure is trying to please everybody.* —Bill Cosby

- *Try not to become a person of success, but rather try to become a person of value.* —Albert Einstein

- *Success comes to those who become success conscious. Failure comes to those who indifferently allow themselves to become failure conscious.* —Napoleon Hill

- *The only place where success comes before work is in the dictionary.* —Vidal Sassoon

- *You can't beat the fog by driving at 90 mph.* —Anon

- *No one can possibly achieve any real and lasting success or get rich in business by being a conformist. —J. Paul Getty*

- *It's easier to get forgiveness for doing something without permission than it is to get permission—especially if you do it well. —Ted Blake*

- *Success does not consist in never making mistakes but in never making the same one a second time.*
  —George Bernard Shaw

- *Good people are good because they've come to wisdom through failure. We get very little wisdom from success, you know. —William Saroyan*

- *When you stay focused and keep a commitment you create momentum, and momentum creates momentum.*
  —Rich Fettke

- *"With your entire 'focus' on your goal, you will reach levels of achievement that you never thought possible.*
  —Catherine Pulsifer

- *The whole secret of a successful life is to find out what is one's destiny to do, and then do it.—Henry Ford*

- *Opportunities don't happen, you create them.*
  —Chris Grosser

- *There are two types of people who will tell you that you cannot make a difference in this world: those who are afraid to try and those who are afraid you will succeed.*
  —Ray Goforth

- *Whenever you see a successful person you only see the public glories, never the private sacrifices to reach them.* —Vaibhav Shah

- *Plan your life like you will live forever, and live your life like you will die the next day.* —Anon

- *One of the most common causes of failure is the habit of quitting when one is overtaken by temporary defeat. Everyone is guilty of this at one time or another.* —Napoleon Hill

- *A man is rich in proportion to the number of things which he can afford to let alone.* —Henry David Thoreau

- *A strong positive mental attitude will create more miracles than any wonder drug.* —Patricia Neal

- *Success is walking from failure to failure with no loss of enthusiasm.* —Winston Churchill

- *I cannot do everything, but I can do something. I must not fail to do the something that I can do.* —Helen Keller

- *Our greatest weakness lies in giving up. The most certain way to succeed is always to try just one more time.* —Thomas A. Edison

- *Successful people rise in the face of criticism.* —Maxwell Maltz

- *Life is 10% what happens to me and 90% how I react to it.* —Charles Swindoll

- *If plan A fails, remember there are 25 more letters in the alphabet.* —Chris Guillebeau

30
FINAL THOUGHTS
AN IMPORTANT DECISION FOR YOU

❖ *When you come to the fork in the road, take it!* —Yogi Berra

There are two fundamental, timeless, and essentially opposite pathways one can take in life, with the objective of achieving personal happiness and fulfilment - and ultimately, one's contentment with one's life when one approaches the end of it. When one realizes this, it is like coming to a fork in the road. For the sake of simplicity, let us call the two paths, Path A and Path B. Each path promises ultimate satisfaction and fulfilment, but each by two very different means. Path A is more about outward material success and Path B is more about inner mastery and spirituality.

Basics of Path A	**Basics of Path B**
Desire is to be encouraged	Desire is to be overcome
Work to improve your situation	Appreciate what you already have
Work to increase your power	Realize you are already powerful
Seeking wealth is a worthy goal	Seeking wealth is often a misguided goal

This book has covered ideas related to both paths, but the one you choose is ultimately up to you. Deciding which path is right for you, may require some soul searching. There are innumerable arguments favouring each path. Advocating one over the other is beyond the scope of this book.

However, we can venture to suggest ways we might resolve this paradoxical dilemma to some extent. For example, one could devote half of one's time to each! One could resolve to devote the earlier portion of one's life to pursuing Path A, and the later part of one's life to Path B. Or one could resolve to spend the first portion of each day pursuing path A and the later portion of each day pursuing Path B, rigorously pursuing material goals until 5.00pm each day, and practicing disciplines belonging to Path B after 5pm, such as meditation, and perhaps reflection on spiritual teachings. Or you could devote three days of the week to one and four days to the other.

Such a balanced approach may have some merit because becoming too obsessively materialistic or too inwardly placid, could both, arguably, have shortcomings, especially when one needs to integrate well with society and the people you care about. It may help to consider who your true role models are and how they approach these things.

It could be argued that all healthy human beings have one ultimate need: to be loved and to love. And to love must surely include the LOVE OF LIFE, not least because this is one type of love that cannot be taken away through loss or bereavement, but only through our own self-programming. And who would want to programme themselves not to love life? So aim to love life! And if that feels impossible at present, then now is the best time to start reprogramming yourself to that end. After all, it's very difficult to be good at anything if you don't enjoy it – and that includes living!

Thankfully, self-mastery and self-reprogramming are available to everyone. In this book, we have shared effective methods. Go forth and take full advantage of them. Today is the first day of the rest of your life!

"I love life and nothing intimidates me anymore."
—Olivia Newton-John

THE BEGINNING
(NOT THE END!)

Congratulations from the Author

Congratulations on reaching the end of this book and the dawn of an amazing new chapter in your life! Your successes will increase as you become adept at applying the ideas we have shared. I urge you to continue implementing and practicing them. Remember to review your A-Log regularly and keep refining your goals. And re-read this book regularly to make sure you are not overlooking anything. I would be privileged to hear how you succeed with the material we've covered. Any suggestions for future editions would also be most welcome. My contact details are below. If you enjoyed this book, please recommend it to your friends. This book would also make a fabulous gift for anyone whose future you care about!

Best wishes for a sensational future!

Alan Ackroyd

PS If you enjoy this book and find it helpful please recommend it to your friends and leave a positive review at the site where you purchased it; it would be truly appreciated. My suggested content of your review would be: (1) what you liked about the book, (2) how it was better than other books you've read and (3) how it helped you.

Thank you!

To contact the Author, please use the message box at: www.fffbook.com, or email AA@FFFbook.com